To: Raymond La Forte

A man who was a
to see through the smoke
and mirrors and see the
TRUTH!

All the best,

Judge J.B. Stevenson 5/9/11

CONDUCT UNBECOMING an Officer and a Lady

"A Case That Will Live In Infamy-

The Conviction of Cadet Webster Smith"

DEDICATION

This book is dedicated to Merle James Smith, the best friend I had as a cadet at the United States Coast Guard Academy (CGA). Without his friendship I may have never graduated from the CGA or entered the National Law Center, George Washington University. He gave me the incentive to endure. And the rest is history.

Table of Contents

PREFACE v

INTRODUCTION 1

CHAPTER 1 6

An American Tragedy 6

CHAPTER 2 9

The Honor Concept 9

CHAPTER 3 20

Before The Court-martial 20

The Article 32 Investigation 26

CHAPTER 4 34

Webster Smith Filed Article 138 Complaint 34

CHAPTER 5 43

The Runaway Jury 43

CHAPTER 6 58

Go Straight To Jail 58

CHAPTER 7 62

The Man Who Perverted Justice At The USCGA 62

CHAPTER 8 66

Who Played The Race Card In The Webster Smith Case?..............................66

CHAPTER 9 73

This Too Will Pass...73

CHAPTER 10 79

No Review, No Comment..79

CHAPTER 11 83

The Aftermath...83

NOTES 91

APPENDIXES 93

Appendix 1 94

A Letter To The Convening Authority 94

Appendix 2 96

A Letter To The Southern Poverty Law Center 96

Appendix 3 99

A Letter To The NAACP 99

Appendix 4 102

The Appeals Begin...102

Appendix 5 103

Webster Smith Appeals The Conviction 103

Appendix 6 104

Letter From Admiral James Van Sice to USCGA Alumni 104

Appendix 7 107

This Is The Ultimate Issue On Appeal As Decided By The Trial Judge, Captain Brian
Judge 107

Appendix 8 113

UNITED STATES COURT OF APPEALS FOR THE ARMED FORCES..................113

Appendix 9 135

Decision of United States Coast Guard Court of Criminal Appeals, With Appendixes . 135

Appendix 10 180

Decision of Court of Appeals for the Armed Forces (CAAF) 180

Appendix 11 207

Appeal to the U. S. Supreme Court For A Writ Of Certiarori (with Appendixes) 207

Appendix 12 255

Amicus Brief in Support of Supreme Court Appeal from U S Army Defense Appellate
Division...255

Appendix 13 270

Decision of Supreme Court Without Comment Denying Certiorari 270

PREFACE

v.

WEBSTER M. SMITH, CADET, U.S. COAST GUARD
FILED UNDER SEAL[*]

MEMORANDUM ORDER AND OPINION FINDINGS OF FACT

During the summer training program at the start of their first class year, Cadet Smith and Cadet [SR] were both assigned to patrol boats that moored at Station Little Creek. Both lived in barracks rooms at the Station...she went on to state that on October 19th....**she agreed to pose for a picture with him in which both of them were nude, and later that night allowed him to perform cunnilingus on her then she performed fellatio on him.**

.... the Government's objection that this evidence is inadmissible in accordance with M.R.E. 413 [sic] is SUSTAINED.

EFFECTIVE DATE
This order was effective on 26 May 2006.
Done at Washington, DC,
/s/
Brian Judge
Captain, U.S. Coast Guard
Military Judge

Article 133. CONDUCT UNBECOMING AN OFFICE AND A LADY:

Any commissioned officer, cadet, or midshipman who is convicted of conduct unbecoming an officer and a lady or gentleman shall be punished as a court-martial may direct. (10 USC Sec. 933)

Sixth Amendment - Rights of Accused in Criminal Prosecutions

In all criminal prosecutions, the accused shall enjoy the right to a speedy and public trial, by an impartial jury of the State and district wherein the crime shall have been committed, which district shall have been previously ascertained by law, and to be informed of the nature and cause of the accusation; to be confronted with the witnesses against him; to have compulsory process for obtaining witnesses in his favor, and to have the Assistance of Counsel for his defense.

INTRODUCTION

I have devoted my life to the pursuit of justice and fairness in America and in the world. As a student of history, a Christian, and as a humanitarian public servant, this case, and the entire process from the court-martial to the Supreme Court decision on appeal offends my sense of justice, human dignity and fairness. When I witnessed with horror the Webster Smith court-martial and appeals, **I saw Justice fall from Heaven as lightning**.

The Webster Smith case was a litmus test for justice in America. Every once in a while a case comes along that puts our humanity as a people, and as Americans, on trial. Everything that we profess to stand for as Americans was on trial. Our sense of justice in America and particularly in the U.S. Military was on trial. This was no ordinary trial. Our humanity was on trial. Our system of justice was on trial. This case dissolved the deceptive façade and exposed certain moral deficiencies in our system of justice. This case alone puts the legitimacy of the entire military justice system at risk.

This was not a rape case. Many senior Coast Guard officers tried to portray it as such. Webster Smith was not and is not a rapist. The court-martial, with all of its faults, proved that this was not a rape case.

1

Rape has occurred at the Coast Guard Academy and onboard the CGC Eagle as far back as 1977. From 1993 until the spring semester of 2005, the Coast Guard Academy (CGA) had 10 officially reported incidents of sexual misconduct, according to information provided by the Coast Guard Academy.

A former female Coast Guard Academy cadet, **Caitlin Stopper**, testified on Capitol Hill and told how her life became an "absolute hell" after she accused a fellow cadet of sexually assaulting her. Ms. Stopper said that Academy officials tried to blame her for the alleged attack. Her attacker was white. He was allowed to quietly resign his cadet appointment. He simply disappeared into the shadows. Her career was ruined; her life has never been the same.

According to a 2008 General Accounting Office Report, from 2003 to 2006 there were NO sexual-harassment complaints at the Coast Guard Academy, but there were 12 incidents of sexual assault reported to the Coast Guard Investigative Service (CGIS), with one incident in 2003, one in 2004, "NONE" in 2005 and 10 in 2006.

The 10 incidents reported in 2006 would appear to have occurred after the Webster Smith court-martial. Webster Smith was removed from the Chase Hall barracks in 2005. Who was doing all of the sexual assaulting in 2006? Why were none of these people brought to justice? They should have been given some form of discipline. It would have made it easier to understand why a general court-martial was necessary to punish Webster Smith.

Before the Webster Smith incident all cases involving allegations of sexual assault were quietly disposed of. The rapists were all allowed to go quietly into the night. None of them were Black. This feeble attempt to make Webster Smith the poster child of Coast Guard Academy sexual assault is not worthy of the traditions of Hopley Yeaton, the first commissioned officer of the Revenue Cutter Service. The Revenue Marines were the forerunners of the modern Coast Guard. Yeaton was the commanding officer of the Revenue Service cutter USRC Scammel. Yeaton probably took along his slave, Senegal, during the Scammel's patrols as this practice was permitted by the Treasury Department at that time. It would appear that the Coast Guard's attitude towards African Americans may have started on March 21, 1791 when Yeaton was commissioned by George Washington. His tomb now lies on the grounds of the Academy. In 1975 the Coast Guard Cadets sailed the USCGC Eagle to Lubec, Maine where Yeaton's remains were exhumed. They were laid to rest at the Coast Guard Academy, not far from Hamilton Hall where Webster Smith was court-martialed.[1]

Webster Smith was not a sexual predator as he was called. He simply refused to stay on his side of the color-line. Apparently, someone felt that a message had to be sent; a lesson had to be taught. Just as East is East and West is West, and never the twain shall meet; the Coast Guard Academy was not going to become a breeding ground for miscegenation.

Until he was court-martialed, Webster Smith was a shining star in American society. He was a success. He had successfully competed for and won an appointment to one of the nation's premier military academies without the help of a congressional appointment. He was a good cadet, a good student, and a top flight athlete. He was six months away from graduating and becoming a commissioned officer in the United States Coast Guard. He was about to become a part of the system; but, out of the blue something terribly tragic happened. He received a wakeup call. He was told in no uncertain terms that his success, his becoming a part of the establishment, did not purchase for him what it purchased for the white cadets; that is, the equal protection of the law.

If this was not a rape case, nor a sexual predator case, then one might be compelled to ask what kind of a case was it. Well, it would appear to be a case of racial profiling. The Coast Guard was

---

[1] Hopley Yeaton, Wikipedia, the free encyclopedia

attempting to make Webster Smith the poster child of Coast Guard Academy sexual assaults. But the profile does not fit.

The Commandant of Cadets, Captain Douglas Wisniewski, addressed the corps of cadets and labeled Cadet Smith a sexual predator. Commander Ronald Bald, the prosecutor at the trial, described him as a manipulative senior who preyed on lonely women. They were attempting to build the profile of the Coast Guard Academy sexual predator. But former Cadet Webster Smith does not fit the profile. Later in this book I will give you the true profile of the Academy's sexual predator.

The Coast Guard Academy trains a group of cadets that others are encouraged to turn to if they are assaulted. Victims can also approach teachers or administrators. They can come forward anonymously or publicly and, according to the school's policies, are offered counseling and guidance whether they choose to have an investigation or not.

This book will tell you what happened. It will tell you who did what to whom; but it will not tell you why. It cannot. The only people who know for certain have not been quoted in any media anywhere that I have been able to discover.

It is left to you the reader to try to fathom why. This book contains all of the relevant facts. Any reasonable person should be able to conclude why Cadet Webster Smith was tried and punished by a General Court-martial. Applying a little bit of common sense and reflecting upon one's own life experiences in America should be sufficient to understand why Webster Smith was targeted.

Finally here is the full story. Now you can see the big picture. Find out who did what to whom, when, where and how. This is a story that is stranger than fiction, more entertaining than a three ring circus. See exactly what the cream of the crop, our nation's best and brightest are doing when they are not making the world safe for democracy. Here are ladies who can out drink, and out party the most salty of sea dogs; and young officer cadets that really know how to let their hair down. When the sun goes down and the lights go out in Chase Hall that is when the real action begins. Here is conduct in the best traditions of hard working, hard drinking, and fast talking seafarers. Here is conduct unbecoming cadets, officers, gentlemen, and ladies.

And at the end of the game, when all the pieces go back into the box, these cadets emerge from the Academy ready to be worthy of the traditions of commissioned officers, gentlemen and ladies, in the service of their country and humanity. Now you can read all about it. The only thing that surprises me about this entire sequence of events is that the United States Coast Guard Academy (USCGA) puts young, healthy, and randy men and women in the same living quarters next door to each other and allows alcohol and drugs to be introduced into that very volatile mixture at social events; and then feigns surprise when these normal human beings do what comes natural.

CHAPTER 1

An American Tragedy

The Webster Smith Story is an American tragedy. It is not just the story of a Black Coast Guard Academy cadet; it is the story of an American family. It is the story of his mother, Belinda; and his father, Cleon; his wife, Lindsey and their daughter; and of his sister and brothers. It is the story of the friends of Webster Smith. They have all been harmed by the violence directed at their son, brother, husband, father and friend.

Webster Smith was born on July 9, 1983 in Houston, Texas. He is the oldest of four children born to Cleon and Belinda Smith. His sister is a senior at the University of Texas at Arlington. The two younger brothers are twins and attended New Mexico Military Institute where one was in the was in the Coast Guard Prep Program. He applied to the Coast Guard Academy but was denied after his brother was court-martialed.

Webster first distinguished himself in the 7th grade when he was inducted into the Honor Society. When he finished the 8th grade he was accepted into the Strake Jesuit Prep School. Before applying to the Coast Guard Academy (CGA) he attended a Navy

Prep school. All of his instructors wrote letters of recommendation strongly in favor of his admission to CGA.

To his classmates, teachers, and coaches at the Coast Guard Academy Webster Smith appeared to be a magnetic, charming and gifted man, who had risen above his circumstances. Yet, in a moment, as if in the twinkling of an eye, a swift series of events diminished his popularity, vilified his name, and assailed his honor. His image was converted by senior Coast Guard officers from a popular athlete and nice guy to that of a sexual predator and public enemy number one at the Coast Guard Academy.

Snatched from his bed in Chase Hall in the middle of the night, he was whisked away to the barracks at the Groton Naval Submarine Base. He became an outcast from his friends and classmates. His dreams of a military career were dashed. He would not graduate from the Coast Guard Academy like his father. He stood up at his court-martial and proclaimed to the world that his greatest wish in life was to be a Coast Guard officer.

Webster had dared to dream some big dreams. Like Alex Haley he had dared to believe that he could rise in the USCG to the highest level to which his talents and initiative could take him. Just like the Tuskegee Airmen and Navy World War II hero, Dorie Miller, he dared to dream that the time had come in America when a Black man could reach his full potential in the military. With energy and vitality he excelled in athletics and academics for three and a half years, before tragedy struck.

His parents were middle class African Americans. His father was a graduate of the Coast Guard Academy in the Class of 1978. There were 28 Black cadets in that class. One of the most distinguished members of that class was Vice Admiral Manson K. Brown, the first African American three star admiral in Coast Guard history.

The Classes of 1977 and 1978 contained the largest numbers of Black freshmen cadets ever to enter the Academy in a single class. The newly created Minority Recruiting Section (G-PMR-3) at Coast Guard Headquarters had traveled the dusty roads of America off the beaten path in search of qualified Black high school graduates who could make good Coast Guard officers. A few extremely gifted Black teenagers were given the chance to demonstrate their gifts. Webster Smith would not be permitted to further that legacy.

His mother, Belinda Ingram Smith, believed in God and a good education. After losing both parents as a teenager, she went on to become the Head Majorette of **Winston-Salem State University** (WSSU) a constituent institution of the University of North Carolina, and a historically Black public research university located in Winston-Salem, North Carolina. She accomplished this in her second year of college, something never before done by a sophomore. She left WSSU before receiving her undergraduate degree and went on to become the first Black female Crime Scene Investigator in the history of the Winston-Salem police Department.

This unbelievable turn about in what had been a Black success story is a singularly American tragedy.

That a cadet so deeply respected and loved by his coaches and classmates could evoke such an outpouring of hate and anger from the senior officers at the Coast Guard Academy is a Coast Guard tragedy and an American tragedy.

CHAPTER 2

The Honor Concept

Unlike the other service academies, admission to USCGA is based solely upon merit and does not require a congressional nomination. Students are officers-in-training and are referred to as cadets. Tuition for cadets is fully funded by the Coast Guard in exchange for an obligation of 5 years active duty service upon graduation. This obligation increases if the cadet chooses to go to flight school or grad school. Approximately 400 cadets enter the academy each summer with about 200 cadets graduating. Graduates are commissioned as ensigns. The academic program grants a Bachelor of Science degree in one of eight majors, with a curriculum that grades cadets' performance upon a holistic education of academics, physical fitness, character and leadership. Cadets are required to adhere to the academy's Honor Concept, "Who lives here reveres honor, honors duty," which is emblazoned in the halls of the academy's entrance.

The Coast Guard Academy Cadet Handbook (2010) tells the new cadet recruit that when you take the oath of office as a Cadet in the United States Coast Guard you begin your development as a commissioned officer in the Armed Forces of the United States. You will be expected to protect and defend the Constitution of the United States and to selflessly serve the American people.

America will place special trust and confidence in your integrity, ability and good character. This special trust and confidence must be earned. Make no mistake, the Academy leadership program is designed to challenge you. Swab Summer will test your self-discipline, your physical stamina, your commitment to service, and your capacity for teamwork. Above all, your success will depend on your daily commitment to the Coast Guard's Core Values of Honor, Respect, and Devotion to Duty.

The first seven weeks at the Coast Guard Academy are referred to as the Swab Summer Training Program. They are a period for training in military fundamentals and physical conditioning. They will prepare the "swabs" to join the Corps of Cadets at the start of the fall semester.

In the Honor Concept there exists a higher standard of conduct that can neither be delineated by laws nor defined by regulations. It is the concept of Honor. Because Coast Guard cadets are called to a life of public service, and desire to attain that special trust and confidence which is placed in our nation's commissioned officers, their actions must be straightforward and always above reproach. As future law enforcement officers, each cadet's word and signature must be regarded as verification of the truth. The Coast Guard Academy's Honor Concept is exemplified by a person who will neither lie, cheat, steal, nor attempt to deceive. It is epitomized by an individual who places loyalty to duty above loyalty to personal friendship or to selfish desire. While the Coast Guard Academy's Honor Concept differs from a code, in that failure to report an honor offense is not itself an honor violation, cadets are required to report all activity that does not incriminate themselves. Moreover, the condoning of an honor violation is a Class I offense under the Cadet Regulations. Disenrollment is a very possible outcome. The Corps of Cadets are stewards of their Honor Concept. The following words are emblazoned in the tiling of Chase Hall's Quarterdeck, the cadet barracks' lobby: Who Lives Here, Reveres Honor, Honors Duty (The Coast Guard Academy Cadet Handbook (2010), p.13)

Military academies and universities across America send millions of young graduates into life each year with their heads stuffed with new ideas, technology, processes, perspectives, and maybe even a little practical experience they can use in their first assignment as newly commissioned officers. Only in a few schools has the person been so fundamentally transformed from the raw material received four years earlier as at a military academy such as the Coast Guard Academy. How does this happen?

When the future cadets arrive for Swab Summer, the vast majority are typical high school graduates. Most of them believe the sun rises and sets on them. By the end of the first week of Swab Summer, they understand this is not the liberal arts college where students wear uniforms they have expected. By the end of Swab Summer they are starting to learn that any value they have in this world is to be earned by their adherence to certain rules of behavior that bind them to each other as Coast Guard cadets and future officers.

At the center of their new world is adherence to a Cadet Honor Code to which they swear: "A cadet will not lie, cheat, or steal, nor tolerate those who do." Their whole new world is shaped around these principles. This initially shapeless reality begins to form into principles of rigid honesty, loyalty to their fellow cadets, and respect for their classmates and all with whom they associate.

Sometime between the end of their first year (Swab Year) and their Second Class Year when they will be expected to indoctrinate the new swabs, the majority start to understand the role of self discipline in riding the emotional waves of adolescence to a more settled understanding that the emotions are as changeable as the sea and not a reliable basis to govern personal behavior. Cadets learn to lead by first learning to follow. Basic Corps Values of honesty and loyalty become their template for acceptability. They develop a new understanding of the guiding role of honesty, truthfulness, and fairness in their world. Until this becomes second nature, a cadet is not prepared to lead, or to defend and to protect the Constitution of the United States of America.

George Washington, John Adams and Abraham Lincoln have all noted in one form or another that, "Our Constitution was made for a moral and religious people. It is wholly inadequate to the government of any other." Until we accept that as a nation, we are destined to continue to flail about rudderless in a tempestuous sea. (Business Ethics Articles From The Honor Code, 2008 by Robert E. Freer, Jr., President, The Free Enterprise Foundation, and Visiting Professor, at The Citadel).

What is conduct unbecoming an officer and a lady? Does it violate the Honor Concept? Does conduct that violates the UCMJ constitute a higher standard than the Honor Concept? Times are changing so rapidly, one wonders if cadets and officers of today can be held to the same standards of conduct that were intended by the drafters of the UCMJ and the MCM promulgated in 1951? Not everyone can be expected to meet ideal moral standards, but how far can the standards of behavior of cadets and officers fall below contemporary community standards without seriously compromising their standing as officers and ladies? Have the changes in ethics and values of American society been reflected in the military?

Men and women behave differently today than they did sixty years ago. They relate differently to each other today than they did sixty years ago. Dishonorable conduct is magnified when it involves interpersonal relationships. Conduct that disgraces an individual personally and compromises her character may render that person unfit to be an officer. Making false statements, appearing intoxicated in public, failing to pay debts, reading another person's mail, using insulting or defamatory language, spreading rumors or gossip about another person, and associating with people known to engage in sexually immoral behavior do not carry the same stigma as they did sixty years ago. Homosexual conduct does not carry the stigma that it did sixty years ago. All of these types of behavior would have constituted behavior punishable by court-martial sixty years ago.

What type of conduct today would violate Article 133 of the UCMJ? Is consensual sodomy a violation of Article 133? Would violation of a cadet regulation be an offense under Article 133? Would engaging in consensual sex with an enlisted member of another branch of the armed forces while on temporary duty be a violation of Article 133 for which a cadet could be punished?

Could breach of a custom of the service result in a violation of Article 133? Many Coast Guard cadet customs have been adopted into the cadet regulations. "Sexual misconduct" at the USCGA is defined as "acts that disgrace or bring discredit on the Coast Guard or Coast Guard Academy and are sexual in nature", including lewd or lascivious acts, indecent exposure or homosexual conduct.

But the definition also includes consensual acts that are prohibited in Chase Hall and on the Academy grounds, such as holding hands, kissing in public or having sex.

There are certain moral attributes common to the ideal cadet, officer, lady and gentleman. If a person commits acts of lewdness, dishonesty, indecency, lawlessness, indecorum, or violation of a cadet regulation that would seriously compromise her standing as a cadet or officer. Such conduct would at the very least be to the prejudice of good order and discipline in the armed forces.

Both the United States Military Academy and the United States Air Force Academy have adopted a **Cadet Honor Code** as a formalized statement of the minimum standard of ethics expected of cadets. Other military schools have similar codes with their own methods of administration. The United States Naval

13

Academy, like the Coast Guard Academy, has a related standard, known as the Honor Concept.

West Point's Cadet Honor Code reads simply that

> **"A cadet will not lie, cheat, steal, or tolerate those who do."**

Cadets accused of violating the Honor Code face a standardized investigative and hearing process. If they are found guilty by a jury of their peers, they face severe consequences, up to and including expulsion from the Academy.

Definitions of the tenets of the Honor Code

LYING: Cadets violate the Honor Code by lying if they deliberately deceive another by stating an untruth or by any direct form of communication to include the telling of a partial truth and the vague or ambiguous use of information or language with the intent to deceive or mislead.

CHEATING: A violation of cheating would occur if a Cadet fraudulently acted out of self-interest or assisted another to do so with the intent to gain or to give an unfair advantage. Cheating includes such acts as plagiarism (presenting someone else's ideas, words, data, or work as one's own without documentation), misrepresentation (failing to document the assistance of another in the preparation, revision, or proofreading of an assignment), and using unauthorized notes.

STEALING: The wrongful taking, obtaining, or withholding by any means from the possession of the owner or any other person any money, personal property, article, or service of value of any kind, with intent to permanently deprive or defraud another person of the use and benefit of the property, or to appropriate it to either their own use or the use of any person other than the owner.

TOLERATION: Cadets violate the Honor Code by tolerating if they fail to report an unresolved incident with honor implications to proper authority within a reasonable length of time. "Proper authority" includes the Commandant, the Assistant Commandant, the Director of Military Training, the Athletic Director, a tactical officer, teacher or coach. A "reasonable length of time" is the time it takes to confront the Cadet candidate suspected of the honor violation and decide whether the incident was a misunderstanding or a possible violation of the Honor Code. A reasonable length of time is usually considered not to exceed 24 hours.

To have violated the honor code, a Cadet must have lied, cheated, stolen, or attempted to do so, or tolerated such action on the part of another Cadet. The procedural element of the Honor System examines the two elements that must be present for a Cadet to have committed an honor violation: the act and the intent to commit that act. The latter does not mean Intent to violate the Honor Code, but rather the Intent to commit the act itself.

Three rules of thumb

1. Does this action attempt to deceive anyone or allow anyone to be deceived?

2. Does this action gain or allow gain of a privilege or advantage to which I or someone else would not otherwise be entitled?

3. Would I be unsatisfied by the outcome if I were on the receiving end of this action?

U.S. Air Force Academy

The Cadet Honor Code at the Air Force Academy, like that at West Point, is the cornerstone of a cadet's professional training and development — the minimum standard of ethical conduct that cadets expect of themselves and their fellow cadets. Air Force's honor code was developed and adopted by the Class of 1959, the first class to graduate from the Academy, and has been handed down to every subsequent class. The code adopted was based largely on West Point's Honor Code, but was modified slightly to its current wording:

> *We will not lie, steal, or cheat, nor tolerate among us anyone who does.*

In 1984, the Cadet Wing voted to add an "Honor Oath," which was to be taken by all cadets. The oath is administered to fourth class cadets (freshmen) when they are formally accepted into the Wing at the conclusion of Basic Cadet Training. The oath remains unchanged since its adoption in 1984, and consists of a statement of the code, followed by a resolution to live honorably:

> *We will not lie, steal or cheat, nor tolerate among us anyone who does.*
> *Furthermore, I resolve to do my duty and to live honorably, so help me God.*

Cadets are considered the "guardians and stewards" of the Code. Cadet honor representatives throughout the Wing oversee the honor system by conducting education classes and investigating possible honor incidents. Cadets throughout the Wing are expected to sit on Honor Boards as juries that determine whether their fellow cadets violated the code. Cadets also recommend sanctions for violations. Although the presumed sanction for a violation is disenrollment, mitigating factors may result in the violator being placed in a probationary status for some period of time. This "honor probation" is usually only reserved for cadets in their first two years at the Academy. (Cadet Honor Code, from Wikipedia, the free encyclopedia)

16

Why have an honor code?

a. In professions such as the military where life is endangered by virtue of the institution's purpose, trust becomes sacred and integrity becomes a requisite quality for each professional. An officer who is not trustworthy cannot be tolerated; in some professions the cost of dishonesty is measured in dollars – in the Army, the cost is measured in human lives. The ability of West Point to educate, train and inspire outstanding leaders of character for our Army is predicated upon the functional necessity of honesty. In short, USMA expects its graduates and cadets to commit to a lifetime of honorable living.

b. In order to foster a genuine commitment to honorable living, USMA maintains Honor as a fundamental value. This value is operationalized through the Cadet Honor Code, the Honor Investigative and Hearing System, and the Honor Education System. Although the Honor Code & System "belongs" to West Point graduates, staff and faculty members, and cadets, the special charter of maintaining the Honor Code & System resides with the Corps of Cadets. Since 1922, the elected members of the Cadet Honor Committee have represented the Corps on all matters pertaining to honor and are the stewards of the Code. (Information Paper on "Honor" – A Bedrock of Military Leadership, USMA at West Point, **MACC-S- HON, 8 May 1998.**)

Spirit of the Code

a. The Cadet Honor Code describes the minimum standard of ethical behavior that all cadets have contracted to live by, not an abstract ideal to strive toward. Easy to understand and meet, it is the expected baseline behavior of cadets, not some ultimate state of purity that is hard to attain.

b. If the Code is the minimum standard for members of the Corps, what is the ideal that cadets should strive for?

c. That ideal is the "Spirit of the Code," an affirmation of the way of life that marks true leaders of character. The spirit of the code goes beyond the mere external adherence to rules. Rather, it is an expression of integrity and virtue springing from deep within and manifested in the actions of the honorable man or woman. Persons who accept the spirit of the code think of the Honor Code as a set of broad and fundamental principles, not as a list of prohibitions. In deciding to take any action, they ask if it is the right thing to do.

d. It is the Spirit of the Code that gives rise to the specific tenets of the Honor Code itself:

The spirit of the code embraces truthfulness in all its aspects. The Honor Code prohibits lying.

The spirit of the code calls for complete fairness in human relations. The Honor Code prohibits cheating.

The spirit of the code requires respect for the person and property of others. The Honor Code prohibits stealing.

The spirit of the code demands a personal commitment to upholding the ethical standards which gird the profession of arms. The Honor Code prohibits toleration of violations.

e. This, then, is the essence of the spirit of the code as it applies to cadets - a cadet is truthful, fair, respectful of others' property, and committed to maintaining ethical standards in the Corps. This spirit shapes not only West Point but sets the ethical standards for leadership in the Army itself.

f. The growth of each cadet as a leader of character is marked by strict adherence to the minimum standards of the code, combined with a driving desire to progress beyond the external standards to an internalization of the spirit of the code. That is expected by the Corps, by the Long Gray Line, and by the nation.

How does the Honor Code operate? (At the U. S. Air Force Academy)

The administration of the Honor Code is accomplished by a joint effort between cadets and Academy officers. Each possible Honor Code violation is thoroughly investigated on the premise that the accused cadet is honorable until a sufficient amount of reasonable evidence shows otherwise. The primary sanction for code violations is dismissal from the Academy. Some cadets, however, are retained on probationary status. The main concern in the administration of the code is that fairness and equity be maintained while teaching the importance of personal responsibility and that the rights of the cadets are fully protected during this process. Cadets are taught the specifics of the administration of the Honor Code during Basic Cadet Training and throughout their Academy experience.

Cadets who live under the Honor Code agree it is a vital part of their development as military professionals. It also represents a broader aspect of ethical maturity which will serve them throughout their lives. As the bearers of the public trust, both as cadets and as officers, it is the Honor Code which helps build a personal integrity able to withstand the rigorous demands placed upon them. (The Honor Code, printable fact sheet, USAFA).

CHAPTER 3

Before The Court-martial

On December 4, 2005 an officer on duty at the United States Coast Guard Academy (USCGA) received an allegation of sexual misconduct from a cadet, setting off an inquiry by the Coast Guard Investigative Services (CGIS), based in Washington, D.C.. (Note 1)

The commandant of cadets, Captain Douglas Wisniewski, took immediate action to initiate an investigation into these allegations.

"Sexual misconduct" at the USCGA is defined as "acts that disgrace or bring discredit on the Coast Guard or Coast Guard Academy and are sexual in nature", including lewd or lascivious acts, indecent exposure or homosexual conduct.

But the definition also includes consensual acts that are prohibited on academy grounds, such as holding hands, kissing in public or having sex.

From 1993 until the spring semester of 2005, the Coast Guard Academy had 10 reported incidents of sexual misconduct, according to information provided by the CGA. Of those, six incidents resulted in dismissal of the accused and two ended in resignation. In the remaining two cases, there was insufficient evidence to pursue charges. No action was taken against the accused.

The Coast Guard Academy had 982 cadets, nearly 30 percent of whom were women in 2005. One out of every three cadets was a female. In the USCGA the torch had passed to a new gender.

Women represent about 30 percent of CGA cadets, compared with less than 20 percent at the Air Force and Naval Academies and about 15 percent at West Point, the Army Academy.

Cadet First Class Webster Smith was charged with sexually assaulting six female cadets in Chase Hall, the cadet living quarters, and in other locations. (Note 2)

Cadet Smith was separated from the corps of cadets after the first complaint was filed on December 4, 2005. He was placed in pre-trial confinement and made to perform hard labor. No charges had been filed against him; but he was confined, forced to work at hard labor on the boat docks during the day, and forbidden to attempt any form of communications with his friends in Chase Hall. He could not go to class to continue his academic studies or eat in the cadet ward room. At night he was transported to the Navy enlisted men's barracks at Groton Naval Submarine Base across the Thames River from the USCGA. (Note 2)

He was not placed in protective custody. No threats had been made against his safety. It was feared that any contact with the potential government witnesses against him would jeopardize the case the Administration was trying to build. No justification was given for these draconian measures.

Smith, a linebacker on the academy's football team, was charged February 9, 2006 under the Uniform Code Of Military Justice (UCMJ) with rape, assault, indecent assault and sodomy with female cadets. He had served about two months of pre-trial confinement before any charges had been preferred against him.

When I first heard that Admiral James Van Sice was considering convening a court-martial to punish a CGA cadet, I was flabbergasted. After much soul searching, I decided to write him a letter.

In my letter to Admiral James van Sice, the Superintendent of the United States Coast Guard Academy, and the man who convened the court-martial that tried Cadet Webster Smith for a long list of sex crimes, this is what I said:

February 2006

Dear Admiral Van Sice,

I think a great travesty of justice has been committed. It appears that a gross miscarriage of justice has been done at the Coast Guard Academy. What I cannot figure out is was it done ignorantly or by design. How do you frame a man, rig a court-martial, and commit the greatest travesty in the history of the Academy in broad daylight with the whole world watching? With bravado, that's how.

The first thing that you do is, you pick the lawyer for the accused. Then you give the lawyer a medal, something of distinction, like the Coast Guard Achievement Medal. And you select someone who was on the Coast Guard Academy board of Control, and someone you appointed to the Board of Directors of the Coast Guard Foundation. You do not want anyone who might be too independent of the Coast Guard Academy. You make sure that you choose someone with broad corporate law experience, someone with broad experience in negotiating and drafting contracts, someone like the former General Counsel for General Dynamic Electric Boat. And you be sure that he has limited or no experience in criminal law, and trial and defense work, someone not very comfortable in a criminal court room.

Then you refuse to give the accused a Coast Guard Detailed Military Counsel, because you know that a Coast Guard lawyer might have too much ethical integrity to go along with the travesty. So, you look around and you find an Individual Military Counsel from the JAG Corps of the Navy. You want someone not familiar with the Coast Guard Rules of Practice and Procedure and the Local Rules. You want someone that you can control, not someone who will swear charges against a prosecution witness who gives self-incriminating testimony at trial without a Grant of Immunity, either Transactional or Testimonial. Also, you need someone who will not ask to see the written Grants of Immunity and have them admitted into the Record as exhibits.

Also, you need someone who will not prepare for the trial. It would not be convenient if he brought a lot of Pre-Trial motions to suppress testimony and Motions In Limine to prevent prosecution behavior that would be prejudicial to the Defendant, like newly commissioned officers being allowed to testify in Ensign uniforms while the accused is wearing cadet garb.

When you schedule the trial is important. In order to give leverage and unfair advantage to the prosecution witness, you wait until after graduation, so that the prosecution has a parade of newly commissioned officers to testify against the cadet.

Then you have to agree not to charge the prosecution witness for crimes against the Uniform Code of Military Justice that you know they committed with Webster Smith. It would be difficult to commit sodomy alone. So both participants would be equally guilty. During their testimony all of the female witnesses gave declaration against their interests and made self-incriminating statements.

And you know that under the UCMJ, anyone can swear charges against anyone else. A seaman can swear charges against an admiral, or a private against a general. Even Webster Smith could swear charges against all of the witnesses against him and those charges have to be disposed of in due process.

That is another reason why you must choose the attorney for the accused very carefully. You do not want him swearing charges against the prosecution witnesses who have no immunity from prosecution. It is still not too late.

Next, at trial you give no Article 31 Warnings. Not a single reporter reported that the witnesses had attorneys or that they were warned. They had to be told that they were suspected of having committed an offense under the UCMJ, that they had a right to remain silent, that anything they said could be used against them in a court of law. Not to warn a person whom you suspect is guilty of a crime under the UCMJ before asking them any questions is a violation of the UCMJ.

Not to put this information before the jury was procedural error. Not one newspaper reported that this information was given to the jurors. If it had been done someone would have reported it. Even non-legal trained reporters know how to report facts whether they seem important to them or not.

If you did what I think you did, you may be subject to charges under the Uniform Code of Military Justice for dereliction of duty. If you did not give the witnesses who testified against Webster Smith grants of immunity, and you allowed them to testify on the record, under oath, and give incriminating statements, without giving them Article 31 warnings, then you have violated the UCMJ. Also, the Defense Team would have had to be given copies of the Grant of Immunity, and the Jury would have had to be told that the witness was testifying under a Grant of Immunity, because that is a factor in judging the credibility of the witness.

Nowhere was it reported that the witnesses came into court with their own lawyers. That would have indicated that they had not been granted immunity from prosecution. Nowhere was it

24

reported that the witnesses were given Article 31 warnings. At least one reporter would have picked up on that. That is a very relevant and important fact.

I cannot believe that you did what I think you did. That would mean that you were running a Three Ring Circus. It may turn out that you guys are the new Gang That Could Not Shoot Straight.

If you allowed those females to testify to things that they engaged in with Webster Smith, things that were violations of the UCMJ, and were not given their own Detailed Military Counsel, and were not given written Grants of Immunity, then they have incriminated themselves and are subject to prosecution under the UCMJ. Since you convened a court-martial to try Webster Smith, then you are duty bound to swear out charges against every woman who testified that she engaged in sodomy, public drunkenness, and conduct unbecoming an officer and gentleperson, among other things.

We are a nation of laws, and Webster Smith was entitled to the equal protection of the law. The Constitution of the United States guarantees him that. When you decided to prosecute him only and not his equally culpable partners for sodomy, you denied him the equal protection of the law. That was a gross violation of his civil rights. Also, if you granted the women immunity and not Webster Smith, then you had better have had a very good reason that will withstand Constitutional scrutiny. Moreover, if you allowed those women to testify under oath, on the record, without any Article 31 warnings, and no grant of full immunity, you placed them in jeopardy. You may have ruined all of their lives.

I am going to allow you and the Commandant (G-L) and Commandant (G-P) time to straighten out this mess. If you do not, I will refer it to the NAACP Legal Defense Fund, Inc. Then I will contact the Congressional Black Caucus, and Webster Smith's senators from Texas, and the Civil Rights Division of the Justice Department to ask them to start an investigation to see if any of Cadet Webster Smith's civil rights were violated.

/s/

L. Steverson

LCDR, U. S. Coast Guard (Retired)

The Article 32 Investigation

The Article 32 Investigation was convened on March 21, 2006 to determine whether there was probable cause to convene a court-martial to prosecute the charges. The Investigating Officer received the testimony of seven female cadets who accused Cadet Smith of assaulting them between May and November 2005.

The USCGA Superintendent, Admiral James Van Sice, was the Convening Authority.

Before cadet Webster Smith could be court-martialed an Article 32 Investigation was required to determine if there was probable cause to believe that a crime under the UCMJ had been committed. It is the military equivalent of a grand jury. **The Article 32 Investigating Officer was Commander Steven Anderson**.

Navy Midshipman Kristin Strizki was among the final witnesses for the government at the Article 32 hearing. Five female Coast Guard Academy cadets, who were alleged victims, testified in secret at the Article 32 hearing. Strizki's testified in public. She testified that the two Coast Guard cadets, Smith and KN, were visiting her in Annapolis, Maryland, when they began drinking at an off-campus house. She said KN passed out after consuming more than 2 liters of wine and two beers. (Note 4)

The next morning, Smith suggested Strizki take her friend to get the morning-after pill, she said.

26

Strizki said her friend had no recollection of having sex with Smith and confronted him.

"He said, 'Oh please, you wanted it,'" she testified. "That's when she said, 'There is no way in hell I would have wanted to have sex with you last night, even if I was sober.'" (Note 4)

Another witness, Coast Guard cadet Jere Cherni, testified that the alleged victim became pregnant and underwent an operation that she felt was immoral. After objections from Smith's attorneys, Cherni was not permitted to specify the operation. (Notes 8, 9)

After hearing all of the evidence, CDR Anderson **made a recommendation to the Convening Authority that the charge of rape NOT be referred to a General Court-martial**. That was like a Grand Jury that refused to indict. It refused to return a true bill of indictment. The District Attorney, at that point, would be foolish to waste the taxpayers' money pursuing charges that were not legally supportable and that he could not prove. The only reason for going ahead in spite of the failure to indict would have been if he had a personal vendetta against the accused or a political motive.

The Article 32 Investigating Officer did not feel that there was sufficient evidence to support the charge. Admiral Van Sice, Captain Wisniewski, and Commander Gill rejected the recommendation of the Article 32 Investigating Officer and referred the charge of rape to a General Court-martial. Admiral Van Sice and Captain Doug Wisniewski were not concerned about wasting the taxpayers' money; nor were they worried about being re-elected. They were secure in their position, and they appear to be blinded by rage and other more revolting motives. They are in a position of public trust, but a reasonable person would have had to question their judgment. All of the cadets at the Academy are in their care for safekeeping and nurturing. They did not hesitate to sacrifice this young cadet for some sinister ulterior motive. Who were they trying to impress?

Judge Paul Weil, a federal administrative law judge who decided many discrimination cases for the Department of Transportation, wrote a long time ago in one of his decision that the Coast Guard has a long history of not dealing fairly with its Black personnel and officers. No one told Webster Smith's parents that before they entrusted their precious son to the Coast Guard Academy's Commandant of Cadets.

The Article 32 Investigating Officer was correct in his assessment. At the Trial Cadet Webster Smith was found **not guilty of raping his girlfriend, Cadet KN.** He was found guilty of extorting sexual favors from **Cadet SR**. These charges were added at the last minute, but Cadet RN **lied** through her teeth. It was alleged that Webster Smith was holding **a secret** over SR that she was afraid would ruin her career if revealed. At the Trial **no one seemed to want to know** what the so-called secret was. Well, the secret was that she was having torrid **sex with a Navy enlisted man** in Virginia the previous summer.

Webster Smith never revealed her secret. He did not even tell his mother and father. They had not been able to speak to him. He was being held off base without any contact with anyone, except his lawyers. **He did not extort SR for sexual favors. She extorted him and lied about it under oath.**

On 19 October 2005 SR sent Webster Smith 3 text messages. Each time she asked him to come to her room. The first time he came to her room, she reminded him of their conversation in Virginia the previous summer, when they fantasized about taking nude photos of each other. Webster did not bring a camera to her room, but she was ready with her camera. They took nude photos of each other with her camera, and he left. There was no touching and there was no sex.

When Webster Smith returned to his room, SR text messaged him a second time, and asked him to come back. When he arrived the second time, SR offered to give him a back massage. When she had finished, he offered to return the favor. They both had their

28

clothes on, but she later alleged that he touched her breast. They did not engage in any sexual acts. Smith went back to his room.

Cadet SR sent him a third text message asking him to come back to her room a third time. She said her legs were sore. Smith massaged her legs and they both got turned on resulting in his performing oral sex on her. When he was finished he stood up to leave. That is when she reached out and grabbed him by his belt and pulled him back to her. She unzipped his fly and took out his penis. He stopped her. He told her that she did not have to do that just because he had serviced her. She said "Yeah, right!" And she proceeded to perform oral sex on him. Then he left.

That does not sound very much like extortion. Extortion should be made of sterner stuff. If SR had been extorted or coerced in any way, why did she call him back two more times? Did she later tell a lie of her own volition or was she coached?

The three sexual encounters occurred in her room on 19 October 2005. Nothing was ever mentioned concerning the events of that night until March of 2006, six months later. When SR was told that her friends needed her help, she told of the events of that night. They told her that they were looking for anyone who had had any sexual involvement with Webster Smith. The events were turned around just enough so that it would seem that Webster Smith had taken advantage of her. He had not. He was a victim of a malicious campaign of lies. A conspiracy had been hatched. The foul deed was in the making. Poor trusting good friend Webster Smith was being duped.

At a Pre-trial hearing, before the Jury was seated, when Cadet SR was called to testify in a motion's session, **she pleaded the 5th Amendment**. She refused to testify on the grounds that she might be incriminated. Later, at trial, she testified, and she lied. No one reported that she was given her Article 31 (right against self-incrimination) Rights, but she testified. What happened between the Pre-trial Hearing and the trial in front of the jury?

Did she make a deal with the Prosecutor and the Convening Authority?

No one reported in any media that she was given a grant of immunity. No written Grant of Immunity was admitted into evidence, or shown to the jury. What happened? Even the lies she told incriminated her.

The charges involving her are the only charges that Webster Smith was found guilty of, except for one other. That was disobedience of an order. The order was not to send any Email messages to his friend at The naval academy at Annapolis, MD.. He sent one Email to his friend. For that he was found guilty of disobedience of an order. That seems awfully petty.

These childish pranks had landed him in jail. The lies of an unscrupulous woman and sending an Email to a friend ended his career and sent him to jail. It ruined a perfect life. He had never received as much as one demerit in his life. All through Navy Prep School he had not received one demerit. All through three and a half years at the Coast Guard Academy, he had not received one demerit. He was on the Regimental Command staff the previous summer.

When he ran afoul of Captain Doug Wisniewski and divulged KN's abortion secret his military career was over. All it took was a few lies, a few innocent but promiscuous young females, and a very angry, ruthless, and powerful captain. This was an abuse of process. To go against the Article 32 Officer's recommendation was an abuse of discretion. To suborn frightened young girls to give biased and slanted testimony was an abuse of the prestige of the Academy. To use the Military Justice apparatus for his own personal vendetta was an abuse of process.

A revealing account in the Navy Times concerning testimony at the trial adds some more background:

Smith's former girlfriend (KN) testified on the opening day of the court-martial that on the night when she and Smith traveled to the Naval Academy at Annapolis she blacked out early and learned the next morning that she and Smith had had sex. Smith told her the condom had broken and recommended she seek emergency contraception, but she did not know whether to believe him, she said.

She also said she couldn't remember details about that morning, including what she was wearing or whether she looked for physical evidence indicating they'd had sex.

Weeks later, she took a home pregnancy test.

> "When did you realize that the accused had actually had sex with you?" asked CDR Ronald Bald, the military prosecutor.

> "When I saw the positive result on the pregnancy test," she said.

> "What did you think had happened?" Bald asked.

> "I thought that I had been date-raped," she replied.

Yet their relationship continued. The night after the rape allegedly occurred, the witness acknowledged, she and Smith attended a concert with friends and then spent the night together in a hotel. (Note 5)

Testimony during pretrial hearings suggested that KN had had an abortion, but the military judge refused to allow any medical records into evidence on June 20, saying it would prejudice the jury. Jurors were told only that KN did not carry the child to term.

Smith and KN remained close even after they returned to the Coast Guard Academy, she said. They continued to exchange affectionate e-mails and continued seeing each other for dinner. Months after the rape allegedly occurred, she said, they had sex in his car. (Note 7)

And while prosecutors say Smith was a controlling, emotionally abusive boyfriend, one of Smith's friends testified that KN was equally to blame.

The friend testified that she was watching a movie with Smith the year before when KN, the girlfriend, walked in and said "How could you do that to me? How could you steal him from me," the witness, Bazinet recalled KN yelling. "It was scary", she testified. She and KN were classmates.

Smith's military defense lawyer, Lt. Stuart Kirkby, stressed there was no DNA, no forensic evidence, no rape kit and no crime scene photos. He said the former girlfriend "doesn't recall anything from the moment she left the house, conveniently, until the very next morning."

Defense attorneys maintained that KN was not as drunk as she said and suggested that she may have concocted the rape accusation to cover up her embarrassment at having sex with an on-again, off-again boyfriend.

When Smith took the witness stand he testified that he and KN had some drinks and went to a bar. She gave him a look, he said, and they went out to the car, where he said they had consensual sex. She got sick after they had sex, he said, but when they got home, she was able to walk to bed. He said they had sex again the next morning and evening. (Note 10)

What began as a trial against an accused sexual predator ended looking more like a series of murky encounters between college students, with consent often clouded by alcohol. But the case also offered a rare and often unflattering glimpse at cadet life.

Two of Smith's four accusers testified that they didn't believe sexual assault was understood or taken seriously enough on campus. Another said she felt alone, unable to explain her situation.

And Capt. Douglas Wisniewski, the departing commandant of cadets, described fear and suspicion in the student body, saying some female cadets were hesitant to come forward with assault allegations _ a culture that Wisniewski spent months denying existed.

"Clearly this needs to be a moment of change at the Coast Guard Academy," said U.S. Rep. Rosa DeLauro, D-Conn., who has proposed a federal review of the school's sexual assault policies. (Note 16)

CHAPTER 4

Webster Smith Filed Article 138 Complaint

Article 138 is one of the most powerful rights under the Uniform Code of Military Justice (UCMJ), but it is one of the rights least known and least used by military personnel. Under Article 138 of the UCMJ, "any member of the armed forces who believes himself (or herself) wronged by his (or her) commanding officer" may request redress. If such redress is refused, a complaint may be made and a superior officer must "examine into the complaint."

Article 138 of the Uniform Code of Military Justice (UCMJ) gives every member of the Armed Forces the right to complain that he or she was wronged by his or her commanding officer. The right even extends to those subject to the UCMJ on inactive duty for training.)

Cadet Webster Smith filed an Article 138 Complaint against Captain Douglas Wisniewski. There is no record of it having been resolved.

ART. 138 of the UCMJ: COMPLAINTS OF WRONGS

> Any member of the armed forces who believes himself wronged by his commanding officer, and who, upon due application to that commanding officer, is refused redress, may complain to any superior commissioned officer, who shall foreword the complaint to the office exercising court-martial jurisdiction over the officer against whom it is made. The officer exercising general court-martial jurisdiction shall examine into the complaint and take proper measures for redressing the wrong complained of; and he shall, as soon as possible, send to the Secretary concerned a true statement of that complaint, with the proceedings thereon.

Article 138 is one of the most powerful rights under the Uniform Code of Military Justice (UCMJ), but it is one of the rights least known and least used by military personnel. Under Article 138 of the UCMJ, "any member of the armed forces who believes himself (or herself) wronged by his (or her) commanding officer" may request redress. If such redress is refused, a complaint may be made and a superior officer must "examine into the complaint."

Article 138 of the Uniform Code of Military Justice (UCMJ) gives every member of the Armed Forces the right to complain that he or she was wronged by his or her commanding officer. The right even extends to those subject to the UCMJ on inactive duty for training.

Matters appropriate to address under Article 138 include discretionary acts or omissions by a commander that adversely affect the member personally and are:

- In violation of law or regulation

- Beyond the legitimate authority of that commander

- Arbitrary, capricious, or an abuse of discretion, or

- Clearly unfair (e.g., selective application of standards).

Procedures for filing complaint

Within 90 days (180 days for the Air Force) of the alleged wrong, the member submits his or her complaint in writing, along with supporting evidence, to the commander alleged to have committed the wrong. There is no specific written format for an Article 138 complaint, but it should be in normal military letter format, and should clearly state that it is a complaint under the provisions of Article 138 of the Uniform Code of Military Justice.

- The commander receiving the complaint must promptly notify the complainant in writing whether the demand for redress is granted or denied.

- The reply must state the basis for denying the requested relief.

- The commander may consider additional evidence and must attach a copy of the additional evidence to the file.

If the commander refuses to grant the requested relief, the member may submit the complaint, along with the commander's response, to ANY SUPERIOR COMMISSIONED OFFICER, who is MANDATED to forward the complaint to the officer exercising General Court-Martial Convening Authority (GCMCA) over the commander being complained about. The officer may attach additional pertinent documentary evidence and comment on availability of witnesses or evidence, but may not comment on the merits of the complaint.

(Special Note: Article 138 clearly states that complaints may be addressed to any superior commissioned officer. However, only the Air Force regulations allow the complainant to bypass their chain of command when filing a complaint. The Army requires that the complaint be filed with the "complainant's immediate superior commissioned officer." A complaint in the Navy or Marine Corps must be submitted "via the chain of command, including the respondent." Before reaching the general court-martial convening authority, an intermediate officer "to whom a complaint is forwarded" may "comment on the merits of the complaint, add pertinent evidentiary material to the file, and, if empowered to do so, grant redress." In the Air Force, the complainant may "submit the claim directly, or through any superior commissioned officer" to the general court-martial convening authority).

GCMCA's Responsibilities

- Conduct or direct further investigation of the matter, as appropriate.

- Notify the complainant, in writing, of the action taken on the complaint and the reasons for such action.

- Refer the complainant to appropriate channels that exist specifically to address the alleged wrongs (i.e., performance reports, suspension from flying status, assessment of pecuniary liability). This referral constitutes final action.

- Retain two complete copies of the file, and return the originals to the complainant.

- After taking final action, forward a copy of the complete file to the Secretary of the Service (i.e., Secretary of the Army, Secretary of the Air Force, etc.), for final approval/disposition.

- The GCMCA is prohibited from delegating his or her responsibilities to act on complaints submitted pursuant to Article 138.

Matters outside the scope of the Article 138 complaint process

- Acts or omissions affecting the member which were not initiated or ratified by the commander

- Disciplinary action under the UCMJ, including non-judicial punishment under Article 15 (however, deferral of post-trial confinement is within scope of Article 138)

- Actions initiated against the member where the governing directive requires final action by the Office of the Secretary of the Service

- Complaints against the GCMCA related to the resolution of an Article 138 complaint (except for alleging the GCMCA failed to forward a copy of the file to the Secretary of the Service)

- Complaints seeking disciplinary action against another

- Situations where procedures exist that provide "the individual notice of an action, a right to rebut, or a hearing" and "review by an authority superior to the officer originating the action." (This includes most administrative boards)

9 MAY 2006

To: Superintendent, U.S. Coast Guard Academy
From: Cadet 1/C Webster Smith
Subj: Article 138 Complaint

1. At about 0200 on 12/4/05 Officers at the direction of the Commandant of Cadets, CAPT Wisniewski entered my room at Chase Hall, took me into custody and removed me to a room in Munro Hall. I was held there,

ordered not to leave and was interrogated by Coast Guard Intelligence Investigators twice over the next several days regarding allegations that I had raped certain female cadets.

2. From the date of my arrest, I was specifically directed not to have contact with other cadets either through personal interaction, telephone or communication via computer. I was forbidden to go to classes but was brought my books such that I could complete remaining work for the academic term.

3. On 12/16/05, I was allowed to go home to Texas on leave with certain restrictions preserved from the earlier conditions, particularly no contact with any of the Corps of Cadets and I was further restricted from coming within 100 miles of the Academy without specific authorization. I continued in that status until February 14, when I returned to New London to face charges for violations of the UCMJ, filed on February 14.

4. It had been my fond hope that I could return to training at the Academy. Discussion, in mid-January, between the Commandant of Cadets and my Father, Cleon Smith, indicated that might be likely. In phone discussions between CAPT Wisniewski, my Father and me on Friday 27, January, the Commandant of Cadets made it very clear that he did not intend on bringing me back to the Academy any time soon. He seemed to attribute that to the investigation on sexual misconduct continuing. When asked, he refused to identify any ways that I was considered a threat to the continuance of that activity but allowed that he did not feel that I would continue with my Academy Class. This was quite disturbing because my Father and I felt that I should be brought under whatever restrictive order and directions as appropriate but I could resume my military duties and

continue my training. CAPT. Wisniewski refused to consider this option. My Father responded that he felt obligated to raise this issue to another level.

5. On my behalf, CDR Merle Smith, USCGR (Ret.) attempted to get an appointment with Admiral Van Sice. CAPT Thomas, the Assistant Superintendent, returned that call on 1 February, 2006. He inquired as to the subject of the desired meeting and CDR Smith's role. CDR Smith identified that he was acting in the role of my counsel. CAPT Thomas expressed concern regarding such a meeting with ADM Van Sice being the Convening Authority, while investigation was being conducted and that he would have to check with the lawyers. CDR Smith pointed out that the Admiral was also the Convening Authority for the purpose of Article 138 complaints and that was the reason for his request. CAPT Thomas said that he would review the matter with the lawyers and get back to him. No further contact was initiated by Academy staff until 8 February, when LT Sanders, my Company Officer called to advise me that charges had been prepared and he would fax them to me.

6. Upon review, we went from no reason for me to be brought back and just sit for some undeterminable period of time (1/27/06), to a request to meet with the Admiral to discuss Article 138 related issues (2/1/06), to 16 counts on 5 Charges (signed 2/9/06). All of this after 60 days of me in limbo but "continuing investigation".

7. I submit that my counsel's attempt to meet with the Superintendent regarding my rights under Article 138 triggered a retaliatory action in the preparation of the ill founded charges against me that were signed on 9 February. I say ill founded because the Convening Authority saw fit to dismiss 10 of the 13 sex related

offenses that were charged, following the recommendation of the Article 32 Investigating Officer. I submit that these charges were crafted to make me appear as a sexual predator and justify my continued separation from the Corps of Cadets and by invoking charges under the UCMJ, preclude me from exercising my rights to complain about the treatment I was receiving from my Commanding Officer. This action was in violation of the law and materially unfair.

8. By this action, I my banished status was continued such that even if I were to be found not guilty of every charge I face I was arbitrarily removed from academic training in December by the Commandant of Cadets and maintained in that status for the entire semester contrary to the provisions of the Academy Regulations. I would also submit that the Naval Academy was able to address these issues without imposing this punishment on the Midshipmen similarly accused of rape, which makes my circumstance appear arbitrary, capricious and an abuse of discretion.

9. On February 16, 2006 the Academy contacted the New London Day newspaper and advised them that I had been charged and a general overview of the charge substance which per further disseminated by the Associated Press and the television networks to the great embarrassment of my parents and public humiliation of both them and me. The Academy had avoided giving information to the media by stating that the matter was under investigation. I fail to see the meaningful distinction regarding public disclosure between pre-charge investigation and the UCMJ mandated Art 32 investigation. I believe that this action was directed by the Commandant of Cadets or at least with his approval. This was continuing mistreatment directed at me,

particularly since 10 of those 16 specifications were dismissed.

10.   The remaining charges and additional charges that have been referred to the GCM will be addressed in that arena but as stated above I feel that I have been wronged by my Commanding Officer as these circumstances have progressed.

/s/
Webster Smith 1/C

There is no record of the disposition of this Article 138 Complaint. If it had been disposed of with proper due process, it is doubtful if the General court-martial would have taken place.

A reliable and well placed source has informed me that the family of former cadet Webster Smith has been unable to get a copy of the disposition of the Article 138 Complaint.

CHAPTER 5

The Runaway Jury

The presumption of innocence is *principle that requires the government to prove the guilt of a criminal defendant and relieves the defendant of any burden to prove his or her innocence. It is* essential to the criminal process. The mere mention of the phrase *presumed innocent* keeps judges and juries focused on the ultimate issue at hand in a criminal case: whether the prosecution has proven beyond a reasonable doubt that the defendant committed the alleged acts. The people of the United States have rejected the alternative to a presumption of innocence—a presumption of guilt—as being inquisitorial and contrary to the principles of a free society.

The Supreme Court has ruled that, under some circumstances, a court should issue jury instructions on the presumption of innocence in addition to instructions on the requirement of proof beyond a reasonable doubt. A presumption of innocence instruction may be required if the jury is in danger of convicting the defendant on the basis of extraneous considerations rather than the facts of the case. That is precisely what happened in the Webster Smith case.

In his opening statement to the Jury Panel on June 26, 2006 the prosecutor, Commander Ronald Bald, described Cadet Smith as a manipulative senior who preyed on lonely women.

Cadet Smith pleaded not guilty in the first court-martial of a cadet in Coast Guard Academy history. The charges ranged from rape, sodomy, and extortion to assault of the female cadets.

He was tried before a jury panel of Coast Guard officers including four white men, one white woman, three Black men and a man of Asian descent. The senior member was a captain with command experience. There were no cadets on the panel. Since there were no cadets on the jury panel, it can truly be asked whether he was afforded the best qualified jury or a jury of his peers. Were the best qualified members appointed to the panel, as the Manual For Courts-martial (MCM) and the UCMJ mandate?

The Uniform Code of Military Justice (UCMJ), (10 USC sec.801 et seq.) supplemented by the Manual For Courts-martial (MCM) provides guidance for a commander empowered to convene a court-martial. The UCMJ and the MCM both contain the following sentence:

"When convening a court-martial the convening authority shall detail as members thereof, such members of the armed forces as, in his opinion, are best qualified for the duty by reason of age, education, training, experience, length of service, and judicial temperament. (UCMJ Art. 25(d)(2)

The MCM specifically states that if it is anticipated that complicated issues of law will be presented before a special court-martial, the convening authority should give consideration to appointing as a member of the court a qualified attorney-at-law. In the Webster Smith case there were no complicated issues of law, but there were some complicated issues of fact. Such being the case, it would have been appropriate for the convening authority to detail at least one first class cadet to the jury panel. The failure to do so prejudiced the case against Webster Smith before the trial started.

In courts-martial constituted similar to the Smith court-martial, I have made the following or a similar argument many times while serving as defense counsel. None of the members of Webster Smith's jury panel had been a cadet at the USCGA while female cadets were living in Chase Hall. Only one had ever attended the USCGA; none had socialized with female cadets; none had attended cadet athletic parties; none had read the cadet regulations; none had counseled a cadet concerning sexual assault; none had first-hand experience with the four class system; none had indoctrinated female cadets; and none had ever had a cadet girl friend. In the unlikely event that any panel member had ever dated a female cadet, chances are that cadet would not have been the first female regimental commander, who got pregnant, had an abortion. A cadet who continued to date Webster Smith, the putative father, for another six months as a cadet while living in Chase Hall. Only after being counseled by Coast Guard lawyers did she come to the conclusion that she might have a credible argument that she might have been raped at some point during her 18 month relationship with the accused. Added to all that was the female rumor mill in Chase Hall that was ringing with the news that Webster Smith was dating another female and he had told her about the Regimental Commander's pregnancy.

If, at least, one cadet had been on that jury, he could have explained to the members during deliberations many of the things that they were completely ignorant of. I contend that the jury did not have a clue as to what living conditions were like in Chase Hall, nor did they know what the social environment was like between Black male upper-class cadets and white female cadets in any of the four classes.

The members who sat on the Webster Smith jury panel probably did not know that cadets are in charge of the day to day affairs in Chase Hall. Cadets run the barracks. Officers are not normally permitted in Chase Hall without a cadet escort. So, many officers might not be aware of the atmosphere that prevails in Chase Hall. It would be difficult for one who has not lived in Chase Hall to put the testimony of a cadet about social happenings into proper perspective.

The cadets in Chase Hall speak a different language than the panel members were familiar with. Here are a few typical examples. In Chase Hall the roommate of a cadet is called his "wife". This was before women were admitted as cadets. An under-class cadet who runs errands for an upper-class cadet is called his "slave", dating back to the days of Hopley Yeaton, the Father of the Coast Guard. Every upper-class cadet has had, at least, two wives and a slave. Ordinary words are given different meanings in the cadet lexicon.

Without an upper-class cadet to resolve ambiguities and to explain simple terms, the members were forced to speculate, assume, and to read between the lines of the testimony that they heard. In all likelihood, they probably did not correctly interpret the testimony given by the cadets at the Webster Smith trial. Without a cadet on the jury panel, the convening authority did not detail the best qualified members in terms of age, experience, training, and judicial temperament.

That being the case, the jury was not composed of the best qualified people available in accordance with the UCMJ and Art 25(d)(2).

Cadet Smith's attorneys raised the possibility that the charges could have been racially motivated. They said they were pleased by the jury's diversity. Cadet Smith is a Black American, but all the accusers were white females.

Cadet Smith's military attorney compared the case to the Salem witch trials, in which people were put to death based on concocted stories that were not backed up by evidence.

With no physical evidence in the case, defense attorneys had hoped to persuade jurors that the testimony of the women was unreliable. There was no DNA evidence, no forensic evidence, no

46

rape kit and no crime scene photos. It was a classic case of "he-said, she-said". It was one cadet's word against another.

Any jury of reasonable men and women would have had a tough time trying to evaluate the credibility of one cadet against another, even though one was a Black man and the other was a white woman. However, the Convening Authority did something subtle but very shrewd. He waited until the white females had graduated from cadet to officer. That made a world of difference at the trial. An officer is as far from a cadet as the East is from the West. It matters little that not more than 24 hours before the officer was herself a cadet. The perception of the jury was that of an officer making an accusation against a cadet. They saw female officers accusing a cadet; they did not see cadet classmates slandering each other. They did not see former lovers getting revenge and pay-back for betrayal of trust.

The defense counsel team failed to try to offset this psychological disadvantage. They let the female officers testify in uniform wearing all that gold. One after another, a parade of white female officers walked in and took the witness stand and lambasted the black cadet. At the very least, all the witnesses should have been required to appear in civilian attire. A Roman Catholic priest would not have been allowed to testify wearing his clerical collar. It would have been highly prejudicial to the accused. It would give the witness extra indicia of truth telling. It would enhance the credibility of the witness in the eyes of the jury, and perhaps even the judge. This is part of the psychology of trying a criminal case.

Cadet Webster Smith had lost the credibility battle before the jury panel retired to deliberate.

Webster Smith took the witness stand and testified at his own court-martial. Normally, it is not a good idea to let the accused testify at his own trial. Cross-examination can be quite vigorous. He enjoys a Constitutional right to remain silent and not to incriminate himself. He is wrapped in a Constitutional presumption of innocence. The Government must prove its case beyond a reasonable doubt. Until that happens, the accused is presumed to be innocent.

The judge must instruct the jury that no adverse inference can be made from the fact that the accused did not testify. However, perhaps because there were so many female officers testifying against Cadet Smith, his defense attorneys may have felt that the volume of the evidence forced them to put their client on the witness stand.

Also, having prosecuted and defended in many court-martials, I know that the average military jury member cares very little about the right of the accused to remain silent, or the right not to testify. They also pay little attention to the judge's instructions not to draw any adverse inferences from the fact that the accused refused to testify. Time after time following a courts-martial I have heard jury members say we wanted to hear what the accused had to say. They say that the accused should testify if he has nothing to hide. Also, they feel that the accused would not be on trial unless he had done something. He may not have committed the acts that he stood accused of, but he must have done something somewhere along the way. He finally had gotten caught. In this case with one female officer after another testifying against a cadet, it was virtually certain that the jury was going to find him guilty of something. The cards were stacked too high against him. In a case of pure "he-said, she-said", it would be a bit difficult to give the jury any portion of "he-said" without the accused taking the witness stand in his behalf. The rules prohibiting the admission of hearsay evidence forced the accused to take the stand.

Only in a court-martial tried by a "judge alone" can an accused be reasonably certain that no adverse inference would be drawn from his refusal to testify. Only then can an accused take a chance on relying upon his constitutionally guaranteed presumption of innocence.

If I had been the lead counsel in this case, I would have requested a trial before a judge alone. In which case, I would only have had to convince one person of the innocence of my client. Or to be precisely correct, I would have had only to convince one person that the Government had not sustained its burden of proof. That is to say, the prosecution had not proven my client was guilty beyond a reasonable doubt. Until that had occurred, my client was still presumed to be innocent. A jury is like a box of chocolate; you never know what you are going to get.

The burden of proof is not on the accused; it is on the prosecution. The burden never shifts. It is always on the Government. The accused is not required to prove his innocence. That is his constitutional guarantee. He is presumed to be innocent.

Commander Ronald Bald, the prosecutor argued that Webster Smith's stories do not make sense and that <u>the defense did not prove</u> that his accusers concocted their stories in a conspiracy against him. That was totally improper and objectionable. He was arguing to the jury that Webster Smith was required to prove his innocence or they should convict him.

The Prosecutor went on to argue to the jury that "The defense hasn't given you a sisterhood. They haven't given you a conspiracy. They haven't given you collusion". This would clearly appear to be prosecutorial misconduct and should have been reversible error. I cannot imagine any instruction from the military judge that would have cured the harm done by such an argument.

That argument alone set the Anglo-American judicial system back more than 200 years. It took American justice back to a time before we had drafted a Constitution, or fashioned a presumption of innocence, or afforded an accused a right not to incriminate himself and to remain silent. It is inconceivable that this mockery of a trial took place in an American court in 2006.

If the defense had tried this case before a judge alone, and if Webster Smith had not testified, based on the testimony adduced at trial, it would have been virtually impossible for the Government to prove its case based on the testimony of SR alone. There was no physical evidence. The case was based on the credibility of the witnesses. If Webster Smith had not put his credibility in issue by taking the witness stand, it is my concerted opinion that the judge would have had to dismiss the charges at the end of the Government's case in chief. It is at that point in a trial that the defense usually makes a motion to dismiss the charges because the Government had not proven all of the elements of the offenses beyond a reasonable doubt.

Moreover, in a trial before a judge alone, I would never have allowed my client to get anywhere near the witness stand. I would have rested my case without calling any witnesses. I would have taken the chance that the judge's oath as a judicial officer to weigh the evidence objectively and fairly would out-weigh his possible human prejudices as a white man.

One may argue that this is Monday morning quarterbacking at its worst. However, now that all of the relevant facts are on the table, it is clear that the Government really had no case. It was counting on Webster Smith to lose the case. That would be like a husband losing an uncontested divorce case. This would explain why the Article 32 Investigating Officer recommended to the Convening Authority that he should not convene a court-martial. The minor charges, like disobeying an order not to try to contact any of his classmates, could have been dealt with at an Article 15 Captain's Mast. That would have constituted non-judicial punishment.

On June 28, 2006 after about eight hours of deliberation, the panel found Cadet Webster Smith guilty of indecent assault, extortion in exchange for sexual favors and sodomy, which in military parlance includes oral sex. All those charges involved only one of the four accusers, SR.

He was acquitted of several charges that stemmed from alleged sexual encounters with the other three female cadets. The defense had argued that the sex was consensual and that the women had colluded against Webster Smith. They were all scorned lovers of one sort or another. Hell has no fury like a woman scorned.

With no physical evidence outside of e-mails and phone records, the trial pitted Smith's version of events against those of his accusers.

Smith was acquitted of all charges involving his conduct with all of the women, except SR. One, his former girlfriend (KN), testified that he raped her after she became intoxicated during a party at the Naval Academy in Annapolis, Maryland. She did not tell them that after she became pregnant and decided to get an abortion, it was Webster Smith who took her to the hospital. He also took care of her and ran errands for her while she convalesced after the abortion. Then he kept their secret for over six months. When he made the fatal mistake of divulging their secret she turned against him.

Smith was found not guilty of the charge that started the investigation. In the course of the investigation information was uncovered that gave rise to other charges. He was found guilty of offenses found during the course of the investigation. He was sentenced to, among other things, six months in jail.

Of the 10 charges referred to the general court martial, Smith was acquitted of one charge of rape, one count of extortion, one count of sodomy, one count of indecent assault and one charge of assault (five of 10 charges). **All findings of guilty cited in the article related to one woman (SR)**. He was also convicted of two other minor military offenses.

However, that is not the full story. The incidents related to Cadet Smith were publicly announced as 16 pending charges in mid-February 2006. These charges related to five women. In early 2006 the Coast Guard Investigative Service (CGIS) undertook an investigation related to yet another woman and Cadet Smith. This resulted in six additional charges, filed in March 2006. The Article 32 Investigation resulted in dismissal of 12 of the 22 charges. This is, **17 of 22 charged allegations were not substantiated (12 dismissals; five acquittals**).

After spending about six months at hard labor and pre-trial confinement, Cadet Smith was sentenced to an additional six months in jail at a Navy brig. No credit was given for the time already served in confinement. In a normal case like this, the six months of pre-trial confinement would have been credited to the sentence adjudged. The accused would not have had to serve any additional time in confinement.

About forty years after Merle James Smith became the first Black American to enter the Coast Guard Academy in 1962, Webster Smith had become the first cadet to be tried by court-martial and sent to jail in 2006. The first female cadets entered in 1976, and they were making enormous strides. Vice Admiral Manson K. Brown, Class of 1978, had been the first Black Regimental Commander. LT Kristen Nicolson, Class of 2006, was the first female Regimental Commander.

Adding female cadets to the cadet barracks at Chase Hall had certainly changed the chemistry within the corps of cadets. Living side by side in the cadet barracks introduced new challenges to the strict military discipline required by the UCMJ, cadet regulations, and the Honor Concept.

Athletic celebrations on and off campus took on a new dimension. Binge drinking and illegal drugs became a staple. Women gave as good as they got. Sexual encounters of every description became common. How many women became pregnant and had abortions we will never know. There was one that we are positive of. She was Webster Smith's girlfriend.

All of the female cadets involved with and associated with Webster Smith escaped clean without any consequences for their actions or their behavior. Mother Nature was the only one who exacted a penalty. Natural Law resulted in a pregnancy. An abortion followed.

If women are equal, they should be treated as equal. Not a single woman was disciplined under the UCMJ or the cadet regulations. All of the female cadets involved in this case graduated and were commissioned as Coast Guard officers. Their testimony at the court-martial painted a picture of female cadets who were untrustworthy, arrogant, and certainly not ladies. **Their conduct was unbecoming an officer and a lady.**

There were many bad decisions made in the course of convening this court-martial. The most regrettable is that it was deemed necessary. Another is that a message has been sent to all future cadets that women have the freedom to act as recklessly as men, yet at the same time they will be immune from consequences.

How can women ever earn the complete respect of their male counterparts when they continually rely upon their gender trump card? They are forever destined to be daddy's girl; always cream puffs with almost the right stuff. This case has shown every cadet that women can get the same privileges as men and not have to shoulder the same responsibilities. The Coast Guard applied a double standard with respect to gender, and a discriminatory standard with respect to race and ethnic origin.

These women were witnesses at a public trial yet they were accorded the equivalent of rape shield protection. This was not a rape case. Not one of the women had been raped. There was testimony of consensual sex acts. Some of the consensual sex acts were unlawful because, among other things, they occurred in Chase Hall, or at Academy functions. How could unlawful consensual sex acts result in charges against only one of the participants? It takes two to tango. **What does it mean for a cadet or a future U.S. military officer to act like a <u>lady</u>? If Webster M. Smith is no gentleman and is unfit to be an officer in the U.S. Coast Guard, then so are the women he was involved with. These women are not ladies and are unfit to be**

commissioned officers. The women in this case should be held accountable to the same standard of conduct.

For a pure ice-water jolt to the senses few juries in recent years have surprised me as much as the Webster Smith court-martial jury. The verdict is in on the jury. We know that, at least, seven of the nine members were brain-dead. One was certifiably insane. This jury said, in essence, we are not concerned about the truth. We can't handle the truth. Just give us enough facts to buttress our predispositions. We can't be bothered with such legal niceties as who has the burden of proof, or whether he has met that burden, or whether all the elements of the offense has been proved beyond a reasonable doubt. Cadet Smith has not proven to us that he did not do it. If he was not guilty of something, then they would not have convened this general court-martial. We are ready to convict based on the prosecution's theory of the case. Pure conjecture, rank supposition, and casual coincidence are enough for us.

It is truly shocking to the conscience how far this jury was prepared to go to ignore the evidence and to send a message to the fleet. You could get more justice from a firing squad than the president of this jury was prepared to give this poor cadet.

Anyone who has not seen "Twelve Angry Men" should run out and buy it. After you have watched it you will have some sense of what the deliberations were like in the Webster Smith case. There was a four-bagger in there, that is a Coast Guard captain, arguing for 5 years of confinement and a $100,000.00 fine; and a two-stripper, that is a lieutenant, pleading for no more than 6 months of confinement. Thankfully this junior officer had the courage of his convictions. After hours of haggling, the jury only awarded 6 months confinement.

The Lieutenant wanted the punishment to fit the crime, but the senior officer wanted to send a message to the fleet that this is how the Coast Guard handles sexual predators. How sad. He sent a message alright. The message was heard loud and clear around the world. The message was that wisdom does not come with age, nor does sound judgment come with rank. The message was that a General Court-martial jury panel was prepared to destroy Cadet Webster Smith and bankrupt his family purely on the disputed and uncorroborated testimony of a coached witness.

It is shocking that some senior officers can exercise such poor judgment. In their reckless rush to send a message to the fleet that this is how the Coast Guard handles sexual predators, they did not want to be confused with the truth that Webster Smith was set-up. Some of the jurors were prepared to sacrifice Mrs. Smith's pride and joy to make a statement. This was to be another first for the Coast Guard.

Not content merely to be the first service academy to admit women, these officers wanted the Coast Guard Academy to be the first to show the world how the Coast Guard will legally and with due process make an example of an innocent cadet.

A mind is a terrible thing to waste, but they wanted to waste the life of Webster Smith to make a point.

The world was not the only ones watching. The corps of cadets was also going to school on what was happening in Hamilton Hall. This was the Doug Wisniewski School of Ethics, and Judgment 101. His concept of military justice more resembles ritual sacrifice. The cadets in Chase Hall saw senior officers recklessly out of control. They saw Captain Doug Wisniewski cannibalizing the cadet corps. Honor was dead. The Honor Code and the Honor Concept was observed more in the breach than at all. Keep your head down and say nothing. All of a sudden it is dog eat dog and every man for himself. In a rat race only the biggest rat can win. Long live King Rat. This is the Legacy of Doug Wisniewski.

Cadet Smith's Dream Team of attorneys raised the possibility that the charges could have been racially motivated. They said they were pleased by the jury's diversity. Cadet Smith is a Black American, but all the accusers were white females.

With no physical evidence in the case, defense attorneys had hoped to persuade jurors that the testimony of the women was unreliable. There was no DNA evidence, no forensic evidence, no rape kit and no crime scene photos. It was a classic case of "he-said, she-said". It was one cadet's word against another.

Any jury of reasonable men and women would have had a tough time trying to evaluate the credibility of one cadet against another, even though one was a Black man and the other was a white woman. However, the Convening Authority did something subtle but very shrewd. He waited until the white females had graduated from cadet to officer. That made a world of difference at the trial. An officer is as far from a cadet as the East is from the West. It matters little that not more than 24 hours before the officer was herself a cadet. The perception of the jury was that of an officer making an accusation against a cadet. They saw female officers accusing a cadet; they did not see cadet classmates slandering each other. They did not see former lovers getting revenge and pay-back for betrayal of trust.

Webster Smith appealed his conviction all the way to the Supreme Court. The U.S. Coast Guard Court of Criminal Appeals scheduled oral arguments in the Case of The Appeal of the Court-martial Conviction of Cadet Webster Smith for January 16, 2008 in Arlington, Virginia.

A legal brief filed by his lawyers claimed the convictions should be thrown out because the defense team was not allowed to fully cross-examine one of his accusers during Smith's court martial. They said that meant the jury didn't hear testimony that the accuser, a female cadet, (SR), had once had consensual sex with a Coast Guard enlisted man and then called it sexual assault.

LCDR Patrick M. Flynn, the government's lawyer for the Coast Guard Court of Criminal Appeals, said 27 November 2008 that the jury "heard enough" and the trial judge was within his rights to impose reasonable limits on the cross-examination.

"They didn't need to hear the additional details the defense is arguing they should have been allowed to hear."

The defense also was asking the court to set aside Smith's convictions on two lesser charges of failing to obey an order and abandoning watch.

CHAPTER 6

Go Straight To Jail

A kangaroo court is a proceeding that denies proper procedure in the name of expediency. It is a fraudulent or unjust trial where the decision has essentially been made in advance, usually for the purpose of providing a conviction. It is also an elaborately scripted event intended to appear fair while having the outcome predetermined from the start. It is a show trial with a reasonable outcome.

As in the case of Webster Smith, it is conducted largely in the open. An accounting of private conduct is done in public. The proceedings appear to be fair, and the sentence is apparently legitimate. The convening authority goes out of its way to be open and fair, but it is nothing more than a show trial. It results in a judicial lynching; such as, Stalin's kangaroo trials of his "enemies", and the Romanian military court which sentenced Nicolae Ceausescu to death.

Associate Justice of the Supreme Court WILLIAM O. DOUGLAS once wrote, "[W]here police take matters in their own hands, seize victims, beat and pound them until they confess, there cannot be the slightest doubt that the police have deprived the victim of a right under the Constitution. **It is the right of the accused to be tried** by a legally constituted court, **not by a kangaroo court**" (*Williams v. United States*, 341 U.S. 97, 71 S. Ct. 576, 95 L. Ed. 774 [1951]).

After his kangaroo court-martial, former Cadet Webster Smith was taken to the U.S. Navy brig at the Submarine Base in Groton, Connecticut on 28 June 2006.

He should have been granted an 8 day deferment of the sentence. This is normally a routine thing. However, this was not a routine case, by any means. Even the vilest military convicted offender is given some time alone with his family to say good-bye. Webster Smith was not. Webster waited in a secure room under double security guards while his written Request for Deferment was presented to Admiral James Van Sice. The Admiral sat in his ivory tower with Commander Sean Gill, his military advisor, and drank coffee. Then he summarily denied the routine request without any justification whatsoever. This has never been done before. Admiral Van Sice received bad advice from his legal advisor.

As soon as Van Sice's signature was on the denial order, two flat-footed agents from the Coast Guard Investigative Service (CGIS) ordered Cadet Smith's parents to vacate the premises. Mild mannered Webster Smith was handcuffed and paraded up and down the corridor like Jesus being paraded between Caiaphas and Pontius Pilate for all the rabble to gawk and marvel. Poor Webster Smith was made a spectacle. Thoroughly humbled and suitably constrained, he was offered for inspection to KN and SR, the two principal witnesses against him. Then, still in handcuffs, he was paraded in front of the news media for a photo opportunity. This was cruel and inhuman punishment. This was truly a new low even for the likes of James Van Sice. This single act more so than preferring groundless charges shows clearly the character of Admiral James Van Sice. His actions indicated that he was not only a racist, and a bigot, but he was also just plain mean spirited.

Originally he was supposed to be transferred on 10 July to a Federal prison for military officers in South Carolina. It did not happen. Admiral Van Sice delayed signing off on the Report of the Court-martial. The delay was not explained. Then plans were to transfer him to the South Carolina prison on 19 July.

Commandant Instruction M5350.4B, The Civil Rights Manual, required the Academy Civil Rights Officer to attempt to resolve informally any civil rights complaint within 5 days of receiving it. Jo Ann Miller, the Academy Civil Rights Officer, planned to retire on 28 July.

To expect this travesty of justice to have a positive effect upon the Coast Guard Academy is tantamount to asking for good fruit to come from a poisonous tree. It will not happen. It will not result in gender equality. It will not make female cadets take responsibility for their own actions. It will not result in more female staff officers at the Academy. Having a female Commandant of Cadets is nice but it is little more than window dressing. It will not turn female coeds at a secular college into female cadets or future Coast Guard officers. It will not cause the Coast Guard to change its policy on releasing the statistics they keep on the number of reported sexual assaults on base.

All of the other military academies have released their statistics on sexual assaults reported. The public has access to those statistics. The Coast Guard has not released the number of assaults reported, or how they were disposed of. There have been many, up to and during the time Webster Smith was in pre-trial confinement. All of the others have been quietly disposed of. From 1993 until the spring semester of 2005, the Coast Guard had confirmed only 10 reported incidents of sexual misconduct, according to information provided by the Coast Guard Academy to the Navy Times. Of those, six incidents resulted in dismissal of the accused and two ended in resignation. In the remaining two cases, there was insufficient evidence to pursue charges. The Coast Guard Academy had 982 students, nearly 30 percent of whom were women at that time.

Only Webster Smith has been persecuted and then prosecuted to the fullest extent possible under the Uniform Code of Military Justice. So far, we have only heard of the most exceptional cases that get reported in the media. The Coast Guard guards its sexual assault statics like the nuclear missile launch codes. It is arguable whether they would release the statistics pursuant to a Freedom of Information Act Request (FOIA). Of course, they would be subject to a subpoena as part of discovery in a discrimination law suit. Or the NAACP Legal Defense, Inc Fund or the Department of Justice could just ask for them. Now that U.S. Representative Rosa DeLauro, D-Conn., has proposed a federal review of the Coast Guard Academy's sexual assault policies and the Government Accounting Office (GAO) is taking closer cognizance of the Coast Guard Academy, I am sure that they will keep a close eye on the statistics.

CHAPTER 7

The Man Who Perverted Justice At The USCGA

The **Case of Webster Smith** spawned investigations, a task force, and the Case of Admiral James Van Sice. The Case of Admiral James Van Sice could have proven to be a most unusual case. It would have been unusual because he could have been charged with **crimes committed in the name of the Law**; that is to say, the Legal PROCESS. Admiral Van Sice and Captain Douglas Wisniewski definitely misused the Legal PROCESS.

This is all the more ironic because these men were the embodiment of what passed for Justice, integrity, and authority at the Coast Guard Academy (CGA). A Task Force appointed by the Commandant, Admiral Thad Allen, and a Special Investigating Flag Officer in the 5th Coast Guard District investigated Admiral Van Sice. This was altogether fitting and proper. This was just as it should have been, because only another Flag Officer, such as an admiral, could know the level of trust and the awesome amount of power that is bestowed upon a man in that position. Only another officer with that many years of experience who had convened courts-martial could know **how much more a court-martial is than just a panel of officers sitting in judgment on a cadet**, or how much more a court is than simply a court room.

It is **a PROCESS**; it is **a spirit**. It is the Palace of Justice. It is **where men expect to be judged fairly** because true Justice is blind.

These men **distorted** and **perverted** justice at the Coast Guard Academy. They **hijacked** the legal PROCESS. They used the military justice system as an instrument of their **personal vengeance**. When they sailed into uncharted waters and convened a court-martial to try a cadet, they **torpedoed Justice** and shattered the illusion of fairness at the Academy. This was a horrendous crime against humanity.

This was nothing less than **dereliction of duty and malfeasance** in office. This was **a conscious betrayal of the oath** that they took to defend and to protect the Constitution of the United States against all enemies, both foreign and domestic.

Van Sice and Wisniewski are, themselves, Coast Guard Academy graduates. Between them they have almost 60 years of experience as Coast Guard officers. They reached maturity over 2 generations ago. They are well educated adults in positions of public trust. They, most of all, should have valued **Justice, Honor, Truth, and Fairness.** They should have been capable of being entrusted with the responsibility for the administration of the PROCESS.

The United States and much of the world watched and waited to see what would be the outcome of this case. This was truly a case without precedent. It is a case that will live in infamy.

Justice was ravished by Admiral Van Sice. We have to re-consecrate the Temple of Justice at the Academy and in the entire U. S. Coast Guard.

The entire Coast Guard was placed on trial when cadet Webster Smith was charged. The **character of every Coast Guard officer** and Academy graduate was placed **in issue** when the Academy Superintendent accused a man of raping his girlfriend 6 months after she had aborted their child and continued a meaningful relationship with him.

Webster Smith was at the beginning of a process that had produced Van Sice and Wisniewski. They were at opposite ends of the pipe line that turns out Commissioned Coast Guard officers. So, the goals and the accomplishments of the Academy were called into question when the two most senior officers at the Academy chose to court-martial a cadet. Even more so, when they chose to ignore the advice of the law specialist they detailed to investigate the charges. That was the Article 32 Investigating Officer who reported to them that the facts would not sustain a conviction for rape. They chose to accept the advice of the Academy staff legal officer over that of the Article 32 Investigating Officer.

A General Court-martial was not necessary to get an accused sent to jail for 6 months. A Special Court-martial could have done that. **This was over-kill**. Even a Summary Court-martial would have been able to send Webster Smith to jail for 30 days. One has to ask what was it that drove these two senior, experienced officers almost mad; so mad, in fact, that they placed their own careers in jeopardy to punish a cadet.

Was it the fact that Webster Smith's girlfriend was the first female Regimental Commander in over 7 years? Or, was it the fact that Doug Wisniewski had handpicked her? Was he secretly in love with her, and had he picked her for Regimental Commander to curry favor with her? Was the fact that she became pregnant by a Black man the ultimate act of infidelity and betrayal to him? Was that why he ordered Webster Smith out of the barracks at Chase Hall to prevent him from being able to talk to her? Was that why he placed him under a restraining order and forced him to work on the boat docks at hard labor many months before a charge sheet was even drafted or a court-martial was even convened?

The Webster Smith case gave the world a microscope to see into the **character of these senior Coast Guard officers.** It gave all of us a chance to look into the character and the values of the men who are charged with the security of the American Homeland. The Coast Guard is the lead agency in the Department of Homeland Security. Are these officers capable of sound judgment? Or do they betray the public trust; or take appropriated funds and buy beer brewing equipment or bar-b-que pits and party while people are suffering?

The big question is HOW! A good start would be to conduct a thorough honest investigation and evaluation of the culture and climate at the Academy. A Task Force has rendered its findings. Regrettably, it did not give a critique of the actions and judgments of all those responsible for the Webster Smith fiasco. The reinstatement of former Cadet Webster Smith and the expunging of his record would be a good start would have been a good start.

Webster Smith has moved on with his life. He is married and has a child. However, he has bad paper that will follow him for the rest of his life. He must register as a sex offender in the State of Texas. A grant of clemency and a Presidential Pardon would be a giant step towards remedying the wrong that has been done.

However, that will not be enough. The **re-consecration of Justice at the Academy** will not be found in a Task Force Report. It will not be found in the Uniform Code of Military Justice, or in the Academy cadet regulations, or in any written documents that no one fully understands or denies. It will have to be found in **the character of the officers and cadets** in the Coast Guard and at the Coast Guard Academy.

CHAPTER 8

Who Played The Race Card In The Webster Smith Case?

Who played the race card in the Webster Smith case? Was it Commandant of Cadets Doug Wisniewski and CWO2 David French? Or was it Webster Smith's defense team? Could it have been the news media? Someone certainly did, because the race of the accused was reported before the trial began.

Excerpts from The Day newspaper said as follows:
Defense lawyers say race is a factor in the case. Smith is black, his accusers are white, and defense attorneys suspect the women conspired to bring false accusations against him.
If race wasn't a factor when six women accused Smith of sexual misconduct, Merle Smith said, it might have been when a seventh woman came forward and the academy added new charges. Most of the sex-related charges have been dismissed.

"...as this thing has continued to evolve, I guess, as the first 16 charges didn't appear to be going well, I guess they had to find another eight to see if they could make that case," Merle Smith said.

Academy officials have said they will not comment on specific allegations before the trial.

The jury of Coast Guard officers included four white men, one white woman, three black men and a man of Asian descent.

Admiral Allen is correct. In his State of the Coast Guard address he said, "We have never been more relevant and we have never been more visible to the Nation we serve".

We are more visible because we have received more publicity. For some people craving recognition, all publicity is good. It is free advertising. Not for an old and venerated service. For an old public service, bad publicity can be dangerous and disastrous.

There was security in our obscurity. Publicity is a blessing and a curse. You can no longer be hidden and presumed to be ethical, and competent. Now you have to demonstrate that competence, and you have to demonstrate the high moral behavior that you claim to have and want to instill in those coming after you. You cannot just talk that talk; now, you have to walk that walk.

The Smith case is the first court-martial of a cadet in the academy's history. The Smith case brought a lot of sudden attention.

The end of Van Sice's military career is more difficult news for the Academy. It has experienced a series of cadet run-ins with the law. The first and most prominent incident happened under Van Sice's watch. He is the father of the Webster Smith debacle. The Commandant of the Coast Guard would have gone a long way toward restoring public faith in the Coast Guard and in the Academy, if he had punished Admiral Van Sice more appropriately and if he had been more forthcoming with the details of his misconduct and the type of punishment.

Smith's attorneys, who raised the possibility that the charges could be racially motivated, said they were pleased by the jury's diversity. Smith is black and the accusers are white.

In a January 21, 2006 article in The Day newspaper it was reported that from 1993 until the spring semester of 2005, the Coast Guard had 10 reported incidents of sexual misconduct, according to information provided by the academy. Of those, six incidents resulted in dismissal of the accused and two ended in resignation. In the remaining two cases, there was insufficient evidence to pursue charges.

One of the other two complaints, stemming from the first semester of 2005-06, resulted in a confession and the Dec. 15 dismissal of a first-year male student, who departed immediately, according to Chief Warrant Officer (CWO) French. He stated that a female cadet reported nonconsensual sexual advances from a freshman male in the Chase Hall barracks, the dormitory where all students reside.

No criminal charges were filed, French said. (Notice he said nonconsensual sexual advances. Is this what CWO French calls rape, when it is done by a white cadet?)

It is safe to assume that none of the male cadets involved were African American, because whenever a Black male is involved the news report very explicitly points out that the male was black, as was reported in the Webster Smith case. Smith, a linebacker on the academy's football team, was charged Feb. 9 under military law with rape, assault, indecent assault and sodomy against female cadets, said CWO David French, an academy spokesman.

The Associated Press reported on February 25, 2006 that a cadet was kicked out instead of prosecuted. (Note 3)

A prosecutor said he was reviewing how information is exchanged with the U.S. Coast Guard Academy after learning a cadet who admitted sexual misconduct wasn't prosecuted but kicked out of school last year.

New London State's Attorney Kevin Kane would not say whether he believes he has jurisdiction in the case.

An academy spokesman said he could not comment on the case, citing privacy rules.

"It was fully investigated and handled appropriately," Chief Warrant Officer David French said.

According to an academy discipline summary, the male cadet was expelled in December after admitting to sexual misconduct that was determined to be nonconsensual.

So, there were 10 reported cases from 1993 to 2005, and not one resulted in a court-martial. The first report of sexual misconduct involving a Black cadet resulted in a General court-martial. It was not just any court-martial, but the type reserved for murder, treason, and assault with intent to commit grievous bodily harm.

The Coast Guard Academy had 982 students, nearly 30 percent of whom were women. If a report involving sexual assault or misconduct is made to the chain of command, CGIS must examine it.

"The commandant of cadets, CAPT Douglas Wisniewski, took immediate action to initiate the investigation into these allegations", CWO2 David French said. French declined a request for an interview with Commandant of Cadets Capt. Douglas Wisniewski. The Coast Guard Academy largely limited its responses to brief written statements delivered by e-mail.

Captain Doug Wisniewski, who graduated from the academy with the last all-male class, was replaced by the first woman to hold the post, Captain Judith Keene, who graduated in the second class to accept women.

"Sexual misconduct at the academy is defined as "acts that disgrace or bring discredit on the Coast Guard or Coast Guard Academy and are sexual in nature", including lewd or lascivious acts, indecent exposure or homosexual conduct. But the definition also includes consensual acts that are prohibited on academy grounds, such as holding hands, kissing in public or sex. This does not include rape, because rape is not a consensual act.

If the Academy disposes of 10 cases of sexual misconduct without a court-martial, but on the 11th case of a report of sexual misconduct it convenes a General court-martial, is that playing the race card? What if all 10 of the first cases involved only white cadets, but the 11th case involved a Black cadet? One has to ask why the Black cadet was singled out for a court-martial.

In the beginning there was the crime of sexual assault at the Coast Guard Academy, and the crime was white on white in Chase Hall. Then darkness moved upon the soul of Douglas Wisniewski, and Doug wanted to paint the face of the crime black. In those days there came a young, charismatic, and well liked cadet named Webster Smith, a cadet greatly favored by the coaching staff and the fairer sex. Webster Smith was a dreamer and he was black. Come now, said Captain Doug, let us slay this dreamer and we will see what happens to his dream of being a Coast Guard officer. So, Wisniewski court-martialed Webster Smith and all the world wondered why.

Is it wrong for Black people to ask if there is a double standard? Would that amount to paranoia on the part of Black people? Or would that be considered playing the race card simply to inquire? Is it absurd to believe that anything more than pure chance resulted in the court-martial of Webster Smith? The fact that he was court-martialed speaks to a social reality that African-Americans are acutely aware of in America. Race is not a card to be dealt, but it determines whom the dealer is and who gets dealt a losing hand. In this case Doug Wisniewski dealt the cards, and he dealt from the bottom of the deck

Whites are generally reluctant to acknowledge racism, but they are quick to accuse Black people of playing the race card. The tendency for whites to deny the extent of racism and racial injustice is reflected in the opinions solicited in Norwich on the day that Webster Smith was found guilty and later sentenced to six months in the brig. White comments were generally that this was a reasonable conclusion to the entire sorry affair. An Academy employee said that this is good. It shows that the Academy took timely and effective action. This was evidence of white denial and total indifference to Black persecution.

Unbelievably, Admiral Van Sice went out of his way to talk to Belinda Smith, Webster Smith's mother, during the trial. He kept assuring her that everything was going to be alright. On several occasions he told her that as soon as the trial was over, everything was going to be alright. For whom? Was Admiral Van Sice in denial or did he think that Belinda and Cadet Webster Smith were expendable?

Perhaps this is why, contrary to popular belief, research indicates that people of color are actually reluctant to allege racism, be it on the job, or in schools, or anywhere else. Far from playing the race card at the drop of a hat, it is actually the case that black and brown folks typically stuff their experiences with discrimination and racism, only making an allegation of such treatment after many, many incidents have transpired, about which they said nothing for fear of being ignored or attacked.

So says Tim Wise, activist, lecturer and director of the new **Association for White Anti-Racist Education (AWARE)**. Tim Wise works from anecdote rather than academic argument to recount his path to greater cultural awareness in a colloquial, matter-of-fact quasi-memoir that urges white people to fight racism 'for our own sake.' Wise is the author of two new books: **White Like Me: Reflections on Race from a Privileged Son** (Soft Skull Press, 2005), and **Affirmative Action: Racial Preference in Black and White**. In White Like Me, Wise offers a highly personal examination of the ways in which racial privilege shapes the lives of most white Americans, overtly racist or not, to the detriment of people of color, themselves, and society.

Precisely because white denial has long trumped claims of racism, people of color tend to underreport their experiences with racial bias, rather than exaggerate them. When it comes to playing the race card, it is more accurate to say that whites are the dealers with the loaded decks.

CHAPTER 9

This Too Will Pass

Former Coast Guard members and others with ties to the Coast Guard Academy were praising the academy's handling of its first court-martial, saying the firm action will help the school's reputation rebound. Many in the region with ties to the academy said the fact the school did not hide the allegations and followed through with a court martial would help its reputation rebound. "The academy has excellent processes in place to deal with this," said John Maxham, Vice President of Development for the Academy Alumni Association. "The most important thing is it was handled in the proper fashion."

Judith Buttery, 50, of Oakdale and a former member of the Coast Guard Band, said the rape allegation was something other colleges and universities have dealt with for years. "It happens so often in every other place," Buttery said. "It's just one of those things the Coast Guard will have to deal with. The Coast Guard Academy will weather this storm."

Chris Morello of Norwich, the Capt. Paul Foyt Chapter co-president of the Coast Guard Academy Parents Association, called the incident disappointing, but was glad the academy handled it well. "It's disappointing for the best of the cadets that work as hard and are dedicated and disciplined to have a few put a black mark on the school," Morello said. "It's not good to judge anything based on one decision or challenge."

I was not one of those praising the Coast Guard Academy for its handling of its first court-martial. It was appalling to me that it should have been a General Court-martial. I agreed with the Article 32 Investigating Officer that the charges could have been resolved at an Article 15 Captain's Mast. Non-judicial punishment would have been more than sufficient.

I felt that a great miscarriage of justice had occurred. The life and career of a very promising cadet had been sacrificed. There were no processes in place to deal with allegations of sexual assault. They were making them up as they went along. This was an experiment. I do not think it will ever happen again.

Fortunately for the family of Webster Smith there were some white knights in the wings watching what I considered a miscarriage of justice and an abuse of process. I am referring primarily to the law firm that took his case on appeal. The case was taken as a pro bono case by the Wilmer Cutler Hale and Dorr law firm.

In December of 2007 as we were waiting for the decision on appeal from the Coast Guard Court of Criminal Appeals, it occurred to me that the best Christmas present the Coast Guard could give to the Lawyers from the Wilmer Cutler Hale and Dorr law firm representing cadet Webster Smith would be to rule against them.

It appeared that the best payment the Law Firm could get for representing Webster Smith would be another chance to make history. Taking this case pro bono, it was obvious that they would not receive any direct financial compensation for their services; but, they already had more money than they can spend.

Far more than money, a chance to make history by arguing the case before the Supreme Court would have been just compensation.

I believed that they had followed this case from day one. They had a premonition of its precedent setting nature. When would another case of this unique nature come along? Not in a thousand years.

Like God up in Heaven, hoping that Pharaoh would not give in and let the Hebrews go free, just so He could give the world repeated displays of his awesome power, Wilmer Cutler Hale and Dorr may have been secretly in its heart of hearts hoping the Coast Guard was as perverse as some had said that they were. That would give Wilmer Cutler Hale and Dorr a chance to make it to the Supreme Court to argue a really very simple and easy case of the wrongful prosecution of the first Black Cadet at the Coast Guard Academy.

Now, that would be a trophy worth more than a million dollar retainer. That would add a modern and impressive new paragraph to their website. They would continue to stroll down the corridors of history as the nation's preeminent civil rights law firm.

Knowing the Coast Guard as I did, I felt reasonably certain that they are about to get the number one item on their Christmas Wish List; that is, a chance to argue before the United States Supreme Court on behalf of a poor Black boy from Texas who had been abused by the military justice system.

Little did I know at the time that the case would be appealed to the Supreme Court, only to have the nation's court of last resort deny the appeal with not one word of explanation.

Could it be that the Court-martial of Webster Smith was just intended to attract media attention? Was Admiral James Van Sice trying to send a message to U. S. Representative Christopher Shays and the Pentagon and the other 3 military academies that this is how the Coast Guard Academy handles sexual assaults?

Former Congressman Shays, from Connecticut, a 10-term incumbent who lost a re-election bid in November 2008, was a conscientious objector during the Vietnam War. He never wore a military uniform. He is a good friend of Richard Blumenthal, a former Democratic senator from Connecticut, who had drawn scrutiny for saying he served in Vietnam when he actually received deferments between 1965 and 1970 and then joined the Marine Reserve.

At the very moment that the court-martial of Webster Smith was underway, U.S. Rep. Christopher Shays, a Connecticut Republican and chairman of the Subcommittee on National Security, Emerging Threats and International Relations, was holding a hearing concerning how officials were handling sexual assault cases in the military and its academies. The Hearings were held in Washington, D.C.. Coast Guard **Rear Admiral Paul J. Higgins from the Coast Guard Academy was on the witness list.**

Military officials said they have worked hard to improve critical areas such as victim support and confidentiality while providing training for all cadets to prevent sexual harassment and assault.

Congress created a task force in 2004 that recommended many such changes. "The Air Force Academy has come a long way in addressing sexual assault and violence since the events of 2003 and before," Brig. Gen. Susan Y. Desjardins, Air Force Academy commandant of cadets, said in prepared testimony.

But Shays suggested that more needed to be done: "We must provide an environment in the military at large that does not condone hostile attitudes and inappropriate actions toward women," Shays said. (Note 17)

It is strangely ironic that in April 2006 Representative Shays hosted a briefing on Capitol Hill where a former female Coast Guard Academy cadet, **Caitlin Stopper**, told of how her life became an "absolute hell" after she accused a fellow cadet of

76

sexually assaulting her. Ms Stopper said that Academy officials tried to blame her for the alleged attack. (Note 16) Her attacker was white. He was allowed to quietly resign his cadet appointment. One has to wonder, if the rapist had been a Black cadet, would he have been allowed to quietly resign; or, would he have received a General Court-martial? That was truly a rape case. The Webster Smith case was not.

And then, along came Webster Smith. He was Black. The age of blaming the alleged victim, apparently was over. Since the academy had excellent processes in place to deal with things like this, it was time to crank up the machinery. The most important thing was that it had to be handled in the proper fashion, but it was time to paint a face on crime at the Coast Guard Academy, that crime being sexual assault. This appeared to be an ideal case for racial profiling. Racial profiling is what happens when you take a set of circumstances associated with a certain crime and used them to identify the type of person likely to commit it.

Rapes have occurred at the Coast Guard Academy or onboard the Academy training ship, USCGC Eagle since as far back as 1977. From 1993 until the spring semester of 2005, the Coast Guard Academy had 10 reported incidents of sexual misconduct, according to information provided by the CGA. If we were to profile all of the sexual assailants from 1977 until the Caitlin Stopper sexual attack, we would get a composite of who should be the poster child for sexual assault at the Coast Guard Academy.

This is what we would get. He would be a white male between the ages of 17 and 21. He would be intelligent and athletic, but he would tend to be an introvert except when he has consumed a small amount of alcohol. Being something of a social misfit, he would prey on lonely or homely girls who solicited his assistance. Typically he would be asked for assistance with homework or with some aspect of an athletic skill that he had excelled at. These situations would tend to lure the unsuspecting female into his orbit of greatest achievement. His superior abilities in these areas would tend to bolster his confidence and give him the courage to mount an assault. Afterwards he would be able to convince himself that she asked for it, or he could fantasize that she came on to him. It was all her fault. He would feel little or no guilt.

According to a 2008 General Accounting Office Report, from 2003 to 2006 there were NO sexual-harassment complaints at the Coast Guard Academy, but there were 12 incidents of sexual assault reported to the Coast Guard Investigative Service (CGIS), with one incident in 2003, one in 2004, "NONE" in 2005 and 10 in 2006.

The 10 incidents reported in 2006 would appear to have occurred after the Webster Smith court-martial. Webster Smith was removed from Chase Hall in 2005. Who was doing all of the sexual assaulting in 2006? Why were none of these people brought to justice? They could have been tried along with Webster Smith.

CHAPTER 10

No Review, No Comment

The **U.S. Supreme Court** has **refused** to hear the **appeal** of Webster Smith. The justices declined to hear the case without comment. The decision of the Court of Appeals for the Armed Forces (CAAF) has become the final decision in the case. (Note 19)

That is a shame because the military justice court-martial and the appeal system is not race neutral. A seemingly race neutral system has operated to deny minority members of the armed forces the equal protection of law. Institutional racism and racial profiling operating in a culture that evolved under the system of slavery have reduced Black appellants to a stereotype and disproportionately predetermines that they will be convicted and that they will not prevail on appeal.

Since the Coast Guard is in the Department Of Homeland Security, Smith has the right to submit additional information to Secretary of Homeland Security Janet Napolitano before she approves his sentence.

Smith also has the right to seek a new trial before the Coast Guard Court of Criminal Appeals. He would have to submit new evidence that has not already been considered in the case. He could also have his record cleaned with a presidential pardon. Since he is a resident of Texas he will have to register as a sex offender.

Most Supreme Court watchers had expected the Supreme Court to hear the case or at the very least to give an explanation of why not.

This case implicated a deep federal circuit conflict regarding the standard of review that applies when a trial judge's restriction on the cross-examination of a prosecution witness is challenged on appeal as a violation of the Confrontation Clause. The Court of Appeals for the Armed Forces (CAAF) held that the standard of review is abuse of discretion rather than de novo. Applying the former standard, the court rejected Webster Smith's Confrontation Clause claim by a vote of 3-2.

The Courts Of Appeals Are Deeply Divided Over What Standard Of Review Applies To Confrontation Clause Claims Like Webster Smith's. The CAAF employed abuse-of-discretion review in resolving Smith's Sixth Amendment challenge to the military judge's restriction on the defense's cross-examination of SR. That approach conflicts with the holdings of five circuits, which consider comparable

Confrontation Clause claims de novo, reserving abuse-of-discretion review for non-constitutional challenges. For example, the Seventh Circuit has stated that "[o]rdinarily, a district court's evidentiary rulings are reviewed for abuse of discretion.

However, when the restriction [on cross-examination] implicates the criminal defendant's Sixth Amendment right to confront witnesses against him, ... the standard of review becomes de novo."

The First, Fifth, Eighth, and Tenth Circuits have adopted the same approach.

Six other circuits, by contrast—the Second, Third, Fourth, Sixth, Eleventh, and District of Columbia Circuits— Take the same approach that CAAF does, applying abuse-of-discretion review even when a restriction on the cross-examination of a prosecution witness is attacked on constitutional grounds. The Sixth Circuit, for example, stated in one case that "[defendant] argues that his right to confrontation was violated when the trial court 'unfairly' limited his cross-examination of [a] government witness .... We review the district court's restriction on a defendant's right to cross-examine witnesses for abuse of discretion."

In short, CAAF's use of an abuse-of-discretion standard in this case perpetuated a clear—and recognized—conflict in the circuits.

The Question Presented Was Recurring And Important, And The Smith Case Was A Good Vehicle For Deciding It.

The circuit conflict at issue warranted resolution by the Supreme Court. The constitutionality of restrictions on cross-examination arises frequently in criminal prosecutions, and in every part of the country. Those cases also show that the conflict over the standard for appellate review of such restrictions is established; there is no benefit to be gained by giving the lower courts additional time to consider the issue. Moreover, the question presented was important, because the standard of review can determine the outcome of an appeal. The difference between a rule of deference and the duty to exercise independent review is much more than a mere matter of degree. In even moderately close cases, the standard of review may be dispositive of an appellate court's decision. That is particularly true when one standard is highly deferential: CAAF, for example, has stated that "the abuse of discretion standard is a strict one," satisfied only when "[t]he challenged action [is] arbitrary, fanciful, clearly unreasonable, or clearly erroneous".

Also, non-uniformity created by the conflict directly affects a fundamental individual right. Some defendants in criminal cases enjoy less protection of the critical right to confront their accusers because of the fortuity of where their trials were held, or, as to cases decided by CAAF, because they have chosen to wear the nation's uniform.

The Webster Smith case presented a good vehicle to resolve the circuit conflict. Webster Smith's standard-of-review argument was both pressed and passed upon in the court of appeals, rendering the issue suitable for review by certiorari. In addition, CAAF's rejection of Smith's argument may well have determined the ultimate outcome. Even applying highly deferential review, CAAF was narrowly divided as to the constitutionality of the military judge's ruling in this case. If even one of the three judges who deemed that ruling not to be an abuse of discretion were to conclude, upon reviewing without deference, that it was inconsistent with the Sixth Amendment, Webster Smith would have prevailed.

Justice truly was not served in this case. American justice has been given a black eye. All American citizens cannot expect the equal protections of the law guaranteed by the United States Constitution. Even those who put on the uniforms of the Armed Forces of the United States of America and swear to defend and to protect the Constitution cannot rely upon its legal guarantees. The Case of Webster Smith is but one grain of sand upon the beaches of American justice. May God save us all from an experience like this at the bar of American justice.

CHAPTER 11

The Aftermath

Webster Smith's faith in American Justice has been shattered. He is simply devastated. The patience of his family has been tested to the limit. His mother and father are coping with serious health related challenges brought on by the stress of this ordeal.

This has been the most serious family crisis that Cleon and Belinda Smith have had to endure. The demands of daily work, uncertainty concerning the future of their son and his little infant daughter due to the consequences of having to register as a sex offender in Texas, the family has put enormous pressure. The family's support network and the friends of Webster Smith have all been stressed to the limit. This has affected their physical and mental health. A simple diet, rest, and exercise have had only minor success in relieving their symptoms.

The simple life style that Belinda and Cleon knew growing up is not available to Webster Smith and his wife and child. Something as simple as a birthday party for their daughter is not available to them. Webster would not be able to attend a party of his daughter and a few of her close friends because of the restrictions imposed by the Texas sex offender law.

Captain Doug Wisniewski, the Commandant of Cadets, graduated from the Academy with the last all-male class. He was transferred to a position at Coast Guard Headquarters in Washington, D.C. and was replaced by the first woman to hold the post, Captain Judith Keene, who graduated in the second class to accept women.

Captain Judith Keene, the first female Commandant of Cadets pledged a tough stance against campus sexual violence in July 2006 following the court-martial in which cadets testified that such issues were not taken seriously. (Note 15)

Such attacks are "just reprehensible and I do not want to graduate a cadet into the Coast Guard as a junior officer who is a perpetrator of sexual assault," said Captain Keene.

The Coast Guard Academy will have the first woman superintendent of a military service academy at the helm of the U.S. C. G. A. when classes convene in the summer of 2011. The commandant of the Coast Guard, Admiral Robert Papp, has selected **Rear Adm. Sandra L. Stosz**, Coast Guard director of reserve and leadership, for the superintendent position. Rear Admiral Stosz **graduated** from CGA in **1982** with a Bachelor of Science degree in Government. She is the first female graduate of Coast Guard Academy to achieve flag rank. Stosz has never married. She states that her Coast Guard career is her lifetime adventure.

No good deed goes unpunished, it had been said. Webster Smith was a keeper of secrets, other peoples' secrets. In the end all the secrets came to light. When they did, there was betrayal of trust and tragedy for all parties to the secrets. Webster Smith kept the secret of KN's pregnancy and abortion during their senior year at the Academy. When he divulged her secret, KN set in motion events that led to his court-martial.

He kept the secret of SR's illicit consensual sex with an enlisted man in Virginia during summer training. That secret led to his conviction.

A study by the Government Accountability Office (GAO) 2008 after a series of revelations about sexual misconduct at U.S. military academies, found that the Coast Guard is not required to report to Congress any measures taken to stem the tide of sexual assault and harassment cases the Coast Guard Academy.

The GAO noted the Coast Guard Academy is the only U.S. military academy not required to report to Congress on sexual-misconduct cases.

> According to the GAO Report, from 2003 to 2006 there were NO sexual-harassment complaints at the Coast Guard Academy, but there were 12 incidents of sexual assault reported to the Coast Guard Investigative Service, with one incident in 2003, one in 2004, "NONE" in 2005 and 10 in 2006.

> The 10 incidents reported in 2006 would appear to have occurred after the Webster Smith court-martial. Webster Smith was removed from Chase Hall in 2005. Who was doing all of the sexual assaulting in 2006? Why were none of these people brought to justice? They could have been tried along with Webster Smith.

> There is something wrong with this picture. The GAO report suggests that CGA's figures may not tell the full story.

> This GAO Report could have been used at the Webster Smith trial. At the very least, it could have been impeachment evidence against Doug Wisniewski, the Commandant of Cadets. He testified concerning an atmosphere of fear among the female cadets because of a sexual predator in Chase Hall.
>
> How could that be? If there were NO reported incidents of

sexual assault in 2005, from whence cometh the atmosphere of fear? If there had been any incidents of sexual assault,, surely they would have been reported, because CAPT Wisniewski was in charge of reporting them.

This same GAO Report could have been used to cross-examine every female who testified against Webster Smith. If any incident had occurred, why did they not report it? Did they forget? Was their memory better at the time of the alleged incident, or later at the court-martial?

Webster Smith was court-martialed in 2006. When was he supposed to have committed these offenses? The Investigation into his conduct began in 2005.
The GAO report suggests that CGA's figures may not tell the full story. That is putting it mildly and politely.

Thirteen female cadets and 11 males at the U.S. Coast Guard Academy (CGA) reported anonymously in an **April 2008 survey** that they experienced **"unwanted sexual contact," ranging from touching to forced sexual acts, during the 2007-08 school year.**

More than three-quarters said that **alcohol or drugs were involved** and that the offender was a fellow cadet.
None of the women sought professional help and only 7 percent discussed the incident with authorities. Not enough of the male respondents answered follow-up questions to provide data, according to the Defense Department survey.
"The fact that we have **cadets who are being predators on cadets** bothers me because I'm committed to giving cadets a safe living and working environment," said **Capt. John Fitzgerald**, the new Commandant of Cadets.

"I'm not going to rest until the day I leave here, working to eradicate that."

The last survey of cadets, done by CGA in October 2006, found that there were 23 incidents of sexual assault involving 14 women and nine men. Cadet focus groups revealed acceptance, and even encouragement, of alcohol use.

A few months before that survey was taken, senior cadet **Webster Smith** was court-martialed on charges of sexual assault, among other things.

The Defense Department conducts a congressionally mandated **"service academy gender relations survey"** every two years at the West Point, Annapolis and the U.S. Air Force Academy. CGA, which falls under the Department of Homeland Security, voluntarily participated last year instead of doing its own survey of cadets.

Participating is a way to make CGA more transparent and to give Coast Guard officials an unbiased look at the state of gender relations at the school, **Fitzgerald** said.

Cadets are told about the survey at a meeting and can choose whether or not to complete it.

It is difficult to draw comparisons between past CGA surveys and the DOD version because the surveys use different terminology, like "sexual assault" versus "unwanted sexual contact," and ask about different timeframes, such as a cadet's entire time at the academy versus one school year.

At the DOD academies, 9 percent of women and 1 percent of men reported experiencing some form of unwanted sexual contact last year, while 52 percent of women and 11 percent of men said they were sexually harassed.

At CGA, 44 percent of women and 14 percent of men reported being sexually harassed. More than three-quarters said the offender was a fellow cadet.

"We can't have sexual harassment here, because you can't be a leader and have people look at you in two different lights," **Fitzgerald** said. "We have to get to a point where if that happens, another cadet will turn around and say, 'Stop. You are a Coast

Guard cadet who will be a Coast Guard officer and you're supposed to be the epitome of a leader and a professional and you can't behave in this manner.' " (Note 21)

Is John Fitzgerald casted from the same mold as Doug Wisniewski? Will he court-martial another cadet?

U. S. Coast Guard COMMANDANT INSTRUCTION 1754.10C (The Sexual Assault Prevention and Response Program) has been promulgated. The purpose of the program is to establish policy and prescribe procedures for the Coast Guard Sexual Assault Prevention and Response Program (SAPRP). The ultimate purpose of this program is to build a culture of prevention, sensitive response and accountability in keeping with the Coast Guard's values of honor, respect, and devotion to duty.

It appears that the message that **the court-martial of Webster Smith** was supposed to send was not received "loud and clear" by the intended parties. Or perhaps the cadets just cannot help themselves. They continue doing what normal, healthy, red-blooded Americans have been doing since the dawn of time.

Could it be that the fault is not with the cadets but with the Administration? If you continue to place these attractive physical specimens in close proximity with each other, and force them to come together as a team, can you really expect them to act any differently? One definition of **insanity is doing the same thing over and over and expecting a different result.**

Civilian colleges do not appear to have the same problems, at least, not to the same degree. At civilian colleges students can inhabit the same physical environment and never really interact. They can remain individuals without developing a group identity. They do not live together, even in a dormitory. No one forces them to take group responsibility for the acts of any individual.

Things are different at a military academy. Strangers are forced to become intimately aware of each other and to work together for a common goal. They bond and they develop a group identity. When one catches a cold, they all sneeze. They begin to take responsibility for each other; they become like family. A little touchy-feely is inevitable.

The most logical solution is to separate the genders. Put them on different floors or in different buildings. It might even be necessary to put them at separate training facilities. That is the only way to eliminate any possibility of unwanted touching. However, eventually they will have to come together for training and for work. That is when the temptations and the infatuations will begin. One person's unwanted sexual contact (sexual assault) can be another person's sexual fantasy. You never know until after the fact.

When Alexander Hamilton organized the Revenue Cutter Service in 1790 it was established in the Department of the Treasury. Later it became known as the Coast Guard. In 1966 it was placed in the Department of Transportation. Today it is the nucleus of the Department of Homeland Security. Webster Smith's case is currently being reviewed for clemency by the Secretary of the Department of Home Land Security, Janet Napolitano.

Webster Smith would have made an excellent military officer. It is Webster Smith and people like him that I want on the wall as our last line of defense for our American way of life protecting us from the great unwashed horde that is coming. Secretary Napolitano who do you want on that wall? Surely not people like former Congressman Christopher Shays, who has never worn the uniform of any branch of the American armed forces. Deferments and conscientious objections will not protect us when the enemy is at the gate. So, I beg you to grant clemency to Webster Smith and recommend a presidential pardon for this abused son of American patriotism.

NOTES

1. Rainey, Richard; AP article, January 21, 2006. Coast Guard Academy Investigating Male Cadet for Sexual Misconduct.

2. Rainey, Richard; AP article, February 17, 2006. Coast Guard Cadet Charged With Rape.

3. Rainey, Richard; AP article, February 25, 2006. Cadet Kicked Out Instead of Prosecuted.

4. Rainey, Richard; AP article, March 21, 2006. Coast Guard Cadet's Rape Hearing Begins.

5. Kime, Patricia, Navy Times, Mar. 27, 2006. *Academy Takes Heat Over Sex-Assault Cases.*

6. Rainey, Richard; AP article, April 13, 2006. Coast Guard Cadet to be Court-Martialed.

7. Rainey, Richard; AP article, June 20, 2006. Coast Guard Cadet's Accuser Testifies.

8. Rainey, Richard; AP article, June 22, 2006. New Witness Testifies in Cadet Rape Trial.

9. Rainey, Richard; AP article, June 26, 2006. Women Describe A Life Of Drinking, Partying And Sexual Favors. Trial Shows Another Coast Guard Academy.

10. Rainey, Richard; AP article, June 26, 2006. The Accused Cadet Takes The Witness Stand.

11. Rainey, Richard; AP article, June 27, 2006. Deliberations Start in Cadet's Rape Trial.

12. Apuzzo, Matt; AP article, July 3, 2006. After The Trial, A Time To Rethink Sexual Harassment Training.

13. New York Times editorial, July 1, 2006. Scandal At The Coast Guard Academy.

14. Manning, Stephen; AP article, July 7, 2006. Academies See Spike In Sexual Offenses.

15. Apuzzo, Matt; AP article, July 12, 2006. Coast Guard Academy Vows to Fight Attacks.

16. Apuzzo, Matt; AP article, February 22, 2006. Coast Guard Academy to Require Females on Sex Assault Cases.

17. CBS/AP News Article, New Haven, CT. December 18, 2006, Congressman Christopher Shays Calls For Investigation Of Sexual Assaults In The Military. CONGRESS TO INVESTIGATE SEX ASSAULTS IN MILITARY.

18. Smith, M. J., The Day, February 20, 2008, The Bottom Line On The Webster Smith Court-martial.

19. Howard, Lee, The Day, Dec. 28, 2010, Supreme Court Won't Hear Appeal In Conviction Of Former CGA Cadet.

20. Ogletree Jr., Charles J; The Presumption of Guilt: The Arrest of Henry Louis Gates Jr. and Race, Class, and Crime in America, Palgrave and Macmillan.

21. Grogan, Jennifer, The Day, CGA official: Inappropriate Sexual Behavior Has No Place at Coast Guard Academy, Jan. 9,2009.

APPENDIXES

Appendix 1

A Letter To The Convening Authority

RADM James C. Van Sice
Superintendent, U. S. Coast Guard Academy
31 Mohegan Avenue
New London, CT. 06320-81003

RE: U. S. v Webster Smith

Dear RADM Van Sice:

I believe a terrible miscarriage of justice occurred upon the conviction of Web Smith, the first in the history of the Coast Guard.

While it's apparent a conviction occurred, what's not apparent is the silence that has occurred among the prosecution and yourself in response to this terrible turn of events.

Having a father in the Merchant Marine for the last Sixty years, my admiration of the Coast Guard has been nothing but respect up until this point.

Please rest assured that more publicity will occur as the public sees exactly what transpired. Please understand that I am upset that you and your staff would be so quick to convict an innocent man. The jury had its hands tied due to the rules that were placed upon them.

While I am not a lawyer, as a Black Disease Intervention Specialist working for a local government, I have seen criminals up close and personal. I know how they think. Mr. Webb is not a criminal. What happened here was jealously, and vengeance by a bunch of old Coast Guard "good old boys" for Mr. Smith dating a bunch of white females.

The entire process from the selection of prosecution to the jury selection was flawed. The only evidence was the word of a couple of incredible females. No physical evidence whatsoever. In essence, a white word against a black word. We know how history reflects the word of a black man, much less in a court martial case with no physical evidence.

The failure of having the females testify before the defense amounts to a military lynching. Not only was Mr. Smith lynched once by having these ridiculous accusations brought against him, but twice by not having the females testify under oath.

Mr. Sice, it takes two to tango. Sodomy, more specifically oral sex has to be a willing give and receive. In my clinic, we see patients receive many sexually transmitted diseases as a consequence of unprotected oral sex. Once again, it takes two to tango. Both are willing participants. It doesn't seem reasonable that Mr. Smith gave oral sex to an unwilling female cadet unless she verbally said no, or physically denied Mr. Smith from going down on her. It appeared that this did not happen.

So, why proceed to convict Mr. Smith without convicting the rest of the female cadets? What's good for goose is not good for the gander? Mr. Sice, please reverse the conviction of this young man, and restore the integrity of the Coast Guard. Go after the real rapists in the academy, not after a bunch of horny cadets.

Best,

████████
Disease Intervention Specialist
SKC Public Health

Appendix 2

A Letter To The Southern Poverty Law Center

July 18, 2006

Mr. Morris Dees
Southern Poverty Law Center
400 Washington Avenue
P.O. Box 5632
Montgomery, AL. 36177-7459

RE: Cadet WEBSTER SMITH-U.S. Coast Guard Academy

Dear Morris,

As a member of the Leadership Council of the Law Center I am writing to ask you to get involved in the Cadet Webster Smith case. The legal team at the Law Center represents those who have no other champion. I have seen the good results that the Center has achieved over the years. I know that you share my passion for truth, justice, and equal justice under the law.

A case of gross injustice and rampant racial discrimination has occurred at the Coast Guard Academy. A graduating senior has been falsely accused, convicted on perjured testimony, and sentenced to six months in jail, expulsion from the Academy, and forfeiture of all pay and allowances. His name is Webster Smith and he is Black. He had been separated from the cadet student body six months before the court-martial and was forced to work on the boat docks. This amounted to essentially a sentence of hard labor before a trial. Moreover, since he is from Houston, Texas, he will have to register as a sex offender. That mark will follow him for the rest of his life, unless we can reverse the

96

conviction.

The Associated Press characterized the trial as follows: "What began as a trial against an accused sexual predator ended looking more like a series of murky encounters between college students, with consent often clouded by alcohol. But the case also offered a rare and often unflattering glimpse at cadet life." (Moment of change' following Coast Guard Academy court-martial By MATT APUZZO Associated Press Writer, July 3, 2006.)

The Superintendent of the Coast Guard Academy has been asked to release Cadet Webster Smith from prison, reinstate him as a cadet, let him finish school, and graduate him with a commission. Our pleas have fallen on deaf ears.

Cadet Webster Smith is a victim of jealousy, racial discrimination, a violation of the 14th Amendment Equal Protection clause, and last but not the least, a victim of a double standard.
He was one of the most loved and respected cadets on campus. But he had two things going against him. One, he had dated the Regimental Commander, and the Dean of Admissions' daughter. Both were white. Since they were white and Cadet Smith was Black, it did not sit well with the Commandant of Cadets. Racial Prejudice is still very much alive at the Academy.

Moreover, when a REAL RAPE case with REAL physical evidence surfaced during Webster Smith's ordeal, Commandant of Cadets, Doug Wisniewski and his staff hushed the case, asked the white cadet to resign quietly and go on his way. NO CHARGES were filed. The real rapist was WHITE!

More facts and background on this case can be found at my web Blog spot at www.cgachasehall.blogspot.com.

I urgently beg you to direct the excellent resources of the Law Center to this case. Just a request for an explanation from the

Superintendent of the Coast Guard Academy would be a tremendous help. Just to get involved with this case will send a loud and clear message that will prevent similar abuses in the future. This case could do a lot to bring positive advertisement and increase respect for the Law Center worldwide. Webster Smith's picture has gone around the word. This case presents you with a fundraising bonanza.

Yours Respectfully,

L. Steverson,

LCDR, USCG (Ret.)

Appendix 3

A Letter To The NAACP

July 17, 2006

Mr. Julian Bond
Chairman, NAACP
National Board of Directors
4805 Hope Drive
Baltimore, MD. 21215-3297

RE: Cadet WEBSTER SMITH- U.S. Coast Guard Academy

Dear Mr. Bond:

This is in furtherance of my letter to you of July 10, 2006 concerning Cadet Webster Smith. He continues to be held in jail. After his court-martial, Cadet Web Smith was taken to the U.S. Navy brig at the Submarine Base in Groton, Connecticut on 28 June 2006. Originally he was supposed to be transferred on 10 July to a Federal prison for military officers in South Carolina. It did not happen, nor has the Admiral signed off on the Report of the Court-martial. The delay has not been explained. The new plans are to transfer him to the South Carolina prison on 19 July. That day might not be accurate either, unless the Admiral intends to deliberately violate Commandant Instruction M5350.4B, The Civil Rights Manual, which requires the Academy Civil Rights Officer to attempt to resolve informally a civil rights complaint within 5 days of receiving it. Joann Miller, the Academy Civil Rights Officer, plans to retire on 28 July. If she lets Webster Smith get out of town before she can attempt an informal resolution, then she will have to spend the remainder of her tour of duty commuting between New London and South Carolina. A copy of the Civil Rights Complaint is attached.

Cadet Webster has not seen or talked to his mother or father since June 28, 2006. They have his power of attorney. They signed the original Complaint.

This is a case of gross injustice and rampant racial discrimination at the Coast Guard Academy. A graduating senior has been falsely accused, convicted on perjured testimony, and sentenced to six months in jail, expulsion from the Academy, and forfeiture of all pay and allowances. His name is Webster Smith and he is Black. He had been separated from the cadet student body six months before the court-martial and was forced to work on the boat docks. This amounted to essentially to a sentence of hard labor before a trial. Moreover, since he is from Houston, Texas, he will have to register as a sex offender. That mark will follow him for the rest of his life, unless we can reverse the conviction.

The Superintendent of the Coast Guard Academy has been asked to release Cadet Webster Smith from prison, reinstate him as a cadet, let him finish school, and graduate him with a commission. Our pleas have fallen on deaf ears.

Cadet Webster Smith is a victim of jealousy, racial discrimination, a violation of the 14th Amendment Equal Protection clause, and last but not the least, a victim of a double standard.

He was one of the most loved and respected cadets on campus. But he had two things going against him. One, he had dated the Regimental Commander, and the Dean of Admissions' daughter. Both were white. Since they were white and Cadet Smith was Black, it did not sit well with the Commandant of Cadets. Racial Prejudice is still very much alive at the Academy.

Moreover, when a REAL RAPE case with REAL physical evidence surfaced during Webster Smith's ordeal, Commandant of Cadets, Doug Wisniewski and his staff hushed the case, asked the white cadet to resign quietly and go on his way. NO CHARGES were filed. The real rapist was WHITE?

More facts and background on this case can be found at my web Blog spot at www.cgachasehall.blogspot.com.

Yours Respectfully,

Judge L. Steverson,

Silver Life Member NAACP

Appendix 4

The Appeals Begin

NOVEMBER 28, 2007

Lawyers for a former cadet who was the first student court-martialed in the 130-year history of the U.S. Coast Guard Academy's are seeking to reverse his convictions for sexual misconduct.

Oral Arguments before the Coast Guard Court of Criminal Appeals is set for 16 January 2008 in Arlington, Va.

Appendix 5

Webster Smith Appeals The Conviction

The U.S. Coast Guard Court of Criminal Appeals has scheduled oral arguments in the Case of The Appeal of the Court-martial Conviction of Cadet Webster Smith for January 16, 2008 in Arlington, Virginia.

A legal brief filed by his lawyers claims the convictions should be thrown out because the defense team was not allowed to fully cross-examine one of his accusers during Smith's court martial. They say that meant the jury didn't hear testimony that the accuser, a female cadet, Shelly Roddenbush (SR), had once had consensual sex with a Coast Guard enlisted man and then called it sexual assault.

LCDR. Patrick M. Flynn, the government's lawyer for the appeal, said 27 November that the jury "heard enough" and the trial judge was within his rights to impose reasonable limits on the cross-examination.

"They didn't need to hear the additional details the defense is arguing they should have been allowed to hear."

The defense also is asking the court to set aside Smith's convictions on two lesser charges of failing to obey an order and abandoning watch.

Appendix 6

Letter From Admiral James Van Sice to USCGA Alumni

Subject: Webster Smith Update

Classmates,

Attached is a note from the new Assistant Superintendent of the Academy, Captain Dan May, '79. All the class correspondents were asked to forward this note to their classmates. I forward it to you without comment.

Many of you have also asked for specific contact info for RADM Van Sice. In the interest of fairness, I have included it as well.

Rear Admiral James C. Van Sice US Coast Guard Academy 31 Mohegan Ave New London, Ct 6320- 8103

James.c.VanSice@uscg.mil

Regards,

XXXXX

Attached is his letter.................

To all CGA Alumni and the Coast Guard Community:

This past January, CAPT Jim Thomas, who then served in my current position as the Assistant Superintendent of the Academy, informed you of a sexual misconduct investigation involving a member of the CGA Corps of Cadets. For those that have continued to follow along the past 6 months, you are well aware that the investigation led to formal charges against a First Class cadet and ultimately a court-martial, the first for an Academy cadet in the history of CGA. I want to take this opportunity to once again reach out to you with some updated information as we continue to move forward and make progress.

Our system of military justice is designed to ensure that all cases are resolved in a just manner. We endeavor to ensure a thorough and professional investigation of allegations brought to the command's attention. The unique facts and circumstances of each case are assessed to determine its appropriate disposition. When a general court-martial is contemplated, an impartial Investigating Officer is selected to assess the evidence and offer recommendations. Accused service members are detailed defense counsel and allowed individual military counsel and/or civilian defense counsel of their choosing. Cases are heard by impartial, qualified court members, before trained Military Judges, in open and transparent proceedings. Fact finders are charged to decide cases weighing the evidence against the high burden of proof imposed on the government. Our commitment to justice, due process and the rule of law requires faithful observance of the processes established by the Rules for Courts-Martial.

Several weeks ago, the CGA court-martial concluded with the First Class Cadet acquitted of five charges (rape, extortion, sodomy, assault and unlawful entry) and convicted of five other charges (extortion, sodomy, indecent assault, attempted failure to obey a lawful order and unauthorized absence). The court-martial members adjudged 6 months confinement, forfeiture of all pay/allowances and dismissal from the service. Although the trial has concluded, the case continues in the post-trial processing phase, which includes the convening authority's (CGA Superintendent) action. After reviewing the results of trial, clemency materials submitted by the defense, and the Staff Judge Advocate's recommendation, the convening authority may disapprove a finding of guilty, and/or approve, disapprove, mitigate or change a punishment (as long as the severity of the punishment is not increased).

The post-trial processing phase can take several months to conclude. While this process unfolds, it is critically important that the convening authority absent himself from engaging in any direct comments concerning the case or the specific outcome.

A case of this nature evokes strong opinion and sentiments among all involved as well as the casual observer. This case has been no exception. Many of you have expressed your views in various venues including emails and letters to CGA. However, until the case is officially resolved, it would be inappropriate for CGA or the convening authority to discuss the particulars of this case in any forum outside
the court-martial process.

Thus, I ask for your continued understanding and patience as this case makes its way towards a final conclusion. Just as Jim did, I also want to reiterate that the Coast Guard Academy is founded on the Coast Guard's core values of Honor, Respect and Devotion to duty. We will never waiver from our commitment to these precious values. We are also committed to the fair treatment of all members of our service.

Just two weeks ago, 274 new cadets reported to CGA, marched onto Washington Parade field and took the oath of service as the Class of
2010. They are some of the best young people our nation has to offer and they are extremely committed to the Coast Guard. They are honored and proud to be at this institution. They are the future of our service. We owe it to them to remain strong and to never waiver from
our service commitments.

v/r, D. R. May, CAPT, USCG Assistant Superintendent U.S. Coast Guard Academy

Appendix 7

This Is The Ultimate Issue On Appeal As Decided By The Trial Judge, Captain Brian Judge

GENERAL COURT-MARTIAL
UNITED STATES COAST GUARD
UNITED STATES
v.
WEBSTER M. SMITH, CADET, U.S. COAST GUARD
FILED UNDER SEAL[*]

MEMORANDUM ORDER AND OPINION
M.R.E. 413 [sic] EVIDENCE CADET [SR]

The Defense has provided notice that it intends to introduce evidence of specific instances of sexual behavior involving then Cadet, now Ensign [SR]. This alleged sexual behavior is the subject of the secret that Cadet Smith is charged with threatening to expose in Specification I of Additional Charge II. The Government seeks to bar the introduction of such evidence pursuant to M.R.E. 412. At the Article 39(a) session held on 23 May 2006, Ensign [SR] did not testify because she invoked her right under Article 31(b) to consult with an attorney. The accused testified as to the content of his conversations with Cadet [SR] on this subject. The Defense also submitted a written statement dated 15 February 2006 that Cadet [SR] provided to the Coast Guard Investigative Service.

FINDINGS OF FACT

During the summer training program at the start

of their first class year, Cadet Smith and Cadet [SR] were both assigned to patrol boats that moored at Station Little Creek. Both lived in barracks rooms at the Station. In May 2005, Cadet Smith approached Cadet [SR] to inform her that he was hearing rumors from the enlisted personnel assigned to the Station that she had a sexual encounter with an enlisted member assigned to the Station. Cadet [SR] told him that this was true, but that it was not a consensual encounter. Cadet Smith then informed the enlisted personnel who were spreading the rumors that the conduct was not consensual.

On or about 19 October 2005, Cadet Smith again approached Cadet [SR]. He told her that he had remained in contact with some of the enlisted personnel assigned to Station Little Creek and that the rumors surrounding her sexual encounter with the enlisted man had continued. This time she told him that the incident with the enlisted man had been a consensual encounter and that scope of the encounter had been greater than she had previously described.

At the Article 32 hearing, Cadet [SR] merely stated that she had confided a secret to Cadet Smith.

In her 15 February 2006 statement, she merely stated that a situation occurred which led to rumors. On both occasions, she went on to state that on October 19th, she was concerned enough that Cadet Smith would expose this secret that **she agreed to pose for a picture with him in which both of them were nude, and later that night allowed him to perform cunnilingus on her then she performed fellatio on him.**

CONCLUSIONS OF LAW

1. Generally, evidence that an alleged victim of a sexual offense engaged in other sexual behavior or evidence of the alleged victim's sexual predisposition is not admissible. M.R.E. 412(a). There are three exceptions to this general rule, but only one

may be relevant here: evidence of the sexual behavior of the victim is admissible if excluding the evidence would violate the constitutional rights of the accused. M.R.E. 412(b)(1)(C). This exception protects the accused's Sixth Amendment right to confront witnesses and Fifth Amendment right to a fair trial. *United States v. Banker*, 60 M.J. 216, 221 (2004). In other words, the accused has a right to produce relevant evidence that is material and favorable to his defense. *Id.* Evidence is relevant if it tends to make the existence of any fact more or less probable than it would be without the evidence. M.R.E. 401. Assuming these requirements are met, the accused must also demonstrate that the probative value of the evidence outweighs the danger of unfair prejudice. M.R.E. 412(c)(3). In this context, the unfair prejudice is, in part, to the privacy interests of the alleged victim. *Banker*, 60 M.J. at 223. M.R.E. 412 is a legislative recognition of the high value we as a society place on keeping our sexual behavior private.

2. The Defense offered several theories of why this evidence is admissible. First, the Defense wanted to introduce this evidence to impeach the credibility of Ensign [SR] when she testifies. The general rule is that a witness' credibility may be attacked in the form of an opinion or by reputation concerning the witness' character for truthfulness. M.R.E. 608(a). Specific instances of conduct of witness may be admitted, at the discretion of the military judge, if probative of truthfulness. I decline to exercise that discretion in this case because I believe that, under these circumstances, the probative value of this evidence is substantially outweighed by the danger of unfair prejudice. Then Cadet [SR] was under no duty to be completely forthcoming with Cadet Smith concerning her private life, particularly under these circumstances since her rumored conduct would be in violation of Coast Guard regulations and could subject her to disciplinary action or other adverse consequences. More important, despite any limiting instruction, members might consider this evidence less for its tendency to prove Ensign [SR]'s character for truthfulness than

for its tendency to prove that she is a bad person. Finally, conflicting testimony on this point from Ensign [SR] and Cadet Smith could easily sidetrack members from testimony regarding the charged offenses which the member's should be focusing on.

3. The Defense also argued that the members must know the substance of Cadet [SR]'s secret in order for them to independently assess whether or not she would feel coerced into taking a nude photograph with Cadet Smith and later engaging in mutual oral sex in order to protect that secret. While the importance of her secret would be relevant in this fashion, I do not think that the members would need to know the specifics. At the Article 39(a) session, the Government offered a generic formulation that would impress upon the members the seriousness of the secret. In essence, the members could be informed that the secret was information that if revealed could have an adverse impact on her Coast Guard career, including possibly disciplinary action under the UCMJ.

4. The final rationale offered by the Defense at the Article 39(a) hearing is the most persuasive. The Defense argued that if the members hear that Cadet [SR] originally told Cadet Smith that a sexual encounter with another man was non-consensual, and then later admitted that it in fact was consensual, then the members could use this testimony to infer that the same thing is happening in this case. In other words, the members could infer that Cadet [SR] has a propensity to bring false accusations against men with whom she has had consensual sexual encounters. I agree that this theory would be a valid reason for admitting this evidence under M.R.E. 412(b)(1)(C), but there are two problems with the Defense proffer. First, the evidence proffered that Cadet [SR] made these statements is not strong since it comes from the accuse d, who has an obvious bias. Cadet [SR]'s written statement and Article 32

110

testimony on this point is not clear. She admitted at the Article 32 that she only partially confided in Cadet Smith in May and fully confided in him on October 19th; however, this is far from proof that she initially claimed that the encounter was non-consensual. In fact, it is consistent with the rest of Cadet Smith's Article 39(a) testimony that on October 19th she told him that the scope of the sexual encounter had been greater than she had previously described. The probative value of this evidence is therefore low.

5. More important, there is no evidence that Cadet [SR] made an official complaint against the unnamed enlisted man. Even if Cadet [SR] told the accused in May that the encounter was not consensual, the nature of this confidential statement is far different from the nature of her statements to law enforcement personnel that she must have known would result in a public prosecution. Cadet [SR]'s alleged statement to Cadet Smith was apparently intended to keep more people from learning about her sexual encounter with the enlisted man. It was not a false complaint to law enforcement. In contrast, her statements made in this case were to law enforcement personal and would certainly lead to a public prosecution. Consequently, even if Cadet [SR] falsely told the accused *in confidence* that her sexual encounter with the enlisted man was nonconsensual *in an effort to suppress rumors*, this would have little value in proving that her *official* allegations against Cadet Smith *resulting in **a public trial*** are also false. I am convinced that the minimal probative value of this evidence is outweighed by danger of unfair prejudice to Ensign [SR]'s privacy interests and the potential danger of sidetracking the member's attention to a collateral issue as described in paragraph 2 above.

For the above reasons, the Government's objection that this evidence is inadmissible in accordance with M.R.E. 413 [sic] is **SUSTAINED**.

EFFECTIVE DATE
This order was effective on 26 May 2006.
Done at Washington, DC,
/s/
Brian Judge
Captain, U.S. Coast Guard
Military Judge

Appendix 8

UNITED STATES COURT OF APPEALS FOR THE ARMED FORCES

UNITED STATES COURT OF APPEALS FOR THE ARMED FORCES

No. 08-0719
Crim. App. No. 1275

UNITED
STATES,
Appellee,

v

WEBSTER M. SMITH, CADET, U.S. COAST
GUARD,
Appellant,

Argued: November 10, 2009
Decided: March 29, 2010

[68 M.J. 445]

[446] STUCKY, J., delivered the judgment of the Court, in which RYAN, J., joined. BAKER, J., filed a separate opinion concurring in the result. ERDMANN, J., filed a separate opinion concurring in part and dis- senting in part, in which EFFRON, C.J., joined.

*

*   *

Judge STUCKY delivered the judgment of the Court.

At trial, the military judge limited Appellant's cross-examination of Cadet SR, the Government's only witness on his three convictions related to sexual mis- conduct. We granted review to decide whether Appel- lant was denied his right to confront his accuser on

114

those three specifications. We hold that Appellant was not denied his right to confront his accuser, and affirm.

I.

A general court-martial consisting of members con- victed Appellant, contrary to his pleas, of attempting to disobey an order, going from his place of duty, sodomy, extortion, and indecent assault. Articles 80, 86, 125, 127, and 134, Uniform Code of Military Justice (UCMJ), 10 U.S.C. §§ 880, 886, 925, 927, 934 (2006). The conven- ing authority approved the sentence the members ad- judged: a dismissal, confinement for six months, and forfeiture of all pay and allowances. The United States Coast Guard Court of Criminal Appeals affirmed on April 9, 2008. *United States v. Smith*, 66 M.J. 556, 563 (C.G. Ct. Crim. App. 2008). Appellant filed a motion for reconsideration which was denied on May 14, 2008. Appellant petitioned this Court for review on July 14, 2008.

II.

As a preliminary matter, the Government contends that Appellant's petition for review was not timely filed, and that therefore the grant of review should be dismissed as improvidently granted. Articl e 67(b), UCMJ, 10 U.S.C. § 867(b) (2006), provides that an ac- cused has sixty days to petition this Court for review from the earlier of "(1) the date on which the accused is notified of the decision of the Court of Criminal Ap- peals; or (2) the date on which a copy of the decision ..., after being served on appellate counsel of record for the accused ... is deposited in the United States mails for delivery by first class certified mail to the accused." In *United States v. Rodriguez*, we held that the sixty-day statutory period for filing petitions for review was jurisdictional and could not be waived. 67 M.J. 110, 116 (C.A.A.F. 2009).

Before filing a petition for review at this Court, Appellant timely sought reconsideration of the CCA's decision. Until the CCA rendered a decision on the re- consideration request, either by denying reconsidera- tion or by granting reconsideration and rendering a new decision, there was no CCA decision for [447] this Court to review.

We hold that Appellant's sixty-day period for filing at this Court began on the date the de- fense was formally notified, under the provisions of Ar- ticle 67(b), UCMJ, of the CCA's decision on reconsid- eration. The evidence of record does not support the Government's contention that the appeal was untimely filed.

III.

Appellant and Cadet SR were cadets at the United States Coast Guard Academy. During the summer of 2005, Cadet SR and Appellant were assigned to neighboring Coast Guard cutters in Norfolk, Virginia. While there, Cadet SR committed an indiscretion that could have jeopardized her ranking as a cadet and threatened her Coast Guard career. Shortly thereafter, Appellant sent her a text message saying that he hoped the rumors he was hearing were not true. Cadet SR discussed the situation with Appellant but lied about some of the details. Appellant "said he'd try to squash rumors, and that it would be okay."

In October of that year, after both had returned to the Academy, Appellant notified Cadet SR that the rumors were persisting. She then truthfully dis- closed the details of her indiscretion.
Appellant said he would continue to try to suppress the ru- mors, but that he needed motivation to do so. Ap-

pellant denied he was seeking sexual favors but suggested the couple take a photograph of them- selves naked together to build "trust in one an- other."

After the photo, Appellant left but re- turned to her room later that evening. On this oc- casion, he inserted his fingers in her vagina and placed his tongue on her clitoris. Cadet SR then performed fellatio on him.

IV.

Appellant alleged that Cadet SR's indiscretion in- volved engaging in sex with an enlisted member and, pursuant to Military Rule of Evidence (M.R.E.) 412(c)(1), Appellant moved to admit evidence of this prior sexual conduct.

That rule provides that "[e]vidence offered to prove that any alleged victim en- gaged in other sexual behavior" is not generally admis- sible. M.R.E. 412(a)(1). However, "evidence the exclu-sion of which would violate the constitutional rights of the accused" is admissible. M.R.E. 412(b)(1)(C).

During a closed hearing conducted pursuant to M.R.E. 412(c)(2), Appellant testified that in May 2005 Cadet SR told him that she had had nonconsensual sex- ual encounters with an enlisted member, but that in Oc- tober 2005 she admitted that those sexual encounters had actually been consensual. Cadet SR invoked her right against self-incrimination and did not testify at the hearing. Appellant argued that he should be al- lowed to question Cadet SR about the encounters for "the specific purpose of establishing a pattern of lying about sexual events."

The military judge sustained the Government's ob- jection to the admission of this evidence, but allowed the "members [to] be informed that [Cadet SR's] secret was information that if revealed could have an adverse impact on her Coast Guard career, including possibly disciplinary action under the UCMJ." The CCA af- firmed this decision. *Smith*, 66 M.J. at 560-61. Appel- lant asserts that the military judge erred in not admit- ting the sexual nature of Cadet SR's indiscretion, and requests that we set aside his convictions for extortion, sodomy, and indecent acts.

V

The Sixth Amendment provides that "[i]n all crimi- nal prosecutions, the accused shall enjoy the right ... to be confronted with the witnesses against him."

U.S. Const. amend VI. The right to confrontation includes the right of a military accused to cross-examine ad- verse witnesses. *See United States v. Clayton*, 67 M.J. 283, 287 (C.A.A.F. 2009). Uncovering and presenting to court members "a witness' motivation in testifying is a proper and important function of the constitutionally protected right of cross-examination." *Davis v. Alaska*, 415 U.S. 308, 316 (1974) (citation omitted).

"Through cross-examination, an accused can 'expose to the jury the facts from which jurors ... could appropriately draw inferences relating to the reliability of the witness.'" [448] *United States v. Collier*, 67 M.J. 347, 352 (C.A.A.F. 2009) (quoting *Davis*, 415 U.S. at 318).

Typically, we review a military judge's decision to admit or exclude evidence for an abuse of discretion. *See United States v. Weston*, 67 M.J. 390, 392 (C.A.A.F. 2009). We have also applied the abuse of discretion standard to alleged violations of the Sixth Amendment Confrontation Clause. *United States v. Moss*, 63 M.J. 233, 236 (C.A.A.F. 2006); *United States v. Israel*, 60 M.J. 485, 488 (C.A.A.F. 2005).

Appellant has the burden under M.R.E. 412 of es- tablishing his entitlement to any exception to the prohibition on the admission of evidence "offered to prove that any alleged victim engaged in other sexual conduct." *United States v. Banker*, 607 M.J. 216, 218, 223 (C.A.A.F. 2004) (citation omitted). To establish that the excluded evidence "would violate the constitutional rights of the accused," M.R.E. 412(b)(1)(C), an accused must demonstrate that the evidence is relevant, mate- rial, and favorable to his defense, "and thus whether it is 'necessary.' " *Id.* at 222 (quoting *United States v. Williams*, 37 M.J. 352, 361 (C.M.A. 1993). The term " 'favorable'" as used in both Supreme Court and mili- tary precedent is synonymous with " 'vital.' " *Id.* (quot- ing *United States v. Valenzuela-Bernal*, 458 U.S. 858, 867 (1982); *United States v. Dorsey*, 16 M.J. 1, 8 (C.M.A. 1983)).

Appellant contends that his inability to cross- examine Cadet SR about the nature of the secret af- fected his convictions for sodomy, extortion, and com- mitting an indecent act. We conclude that further cross-examination of Cadet SR was not "constitution- ally required." Assuming arguendo that the exact na- ture of the indiscretion—that it involved consensual sexual relations with an enlisted member—was rele- vant, it was neither material nor vital to Appellant's defense.

Testimony is material if it was " 'of consequence to the determination of' appellant's guilt." *Dorsey*, 16 M.J. at 6 (quoting M.R.E. 401). In determining whether evi- dence is of consequence to the determination of Appel- lant's guilt, we "consider the importance of the issue for which the evidence was offered in relation to the other issues in this case; the extent to which this issue is in dispute; and the nature of other evidence in the case pertaining to this issue." *Id.* (citation omitted). In this case, the evidence was offered on a significant issue, the alleged victim's credibility, which was in dispute. Nev- ertheless, knowledge of the exact nature of her indis- cretion in relation to the other issues in the case was not important. The military judge allowed Appellant to present a fairly precise and plausible theory of bias, i.e., that she lied to preserve a secret which "if revealed could have an adverse impact on her Coast Guard ca- reer, including possibly disciplinary action under the UCMJ." While Cadet SR's credibility was in conten- tion, it is unclear why the lurid nuances of her sexual past would have added much to Appellant's extant the- ory of fabrication.

Nor is cross-examining Cadet SR about her sexual past "'vital'" under *Banker,* 60 M.J. at 222 (quoting *Valenzuela-Bernal,* 458 U.S. at 867; *Dorsey,* 16 M.J. at 8). The "vital" issue is not whether Cadet SR engaged in consensual sex with an enlisted member or whether she lied to Appellant about it, but rather whether she lied about an important issue that would impeach her credibility. Cadet SR admitted that she had been in a "situation" that could have jeopardized her career and her ranking as a cadet; that the "situation" was in viola- tion of cadet regulations and possibly a violation of the UCMJ; and that she initially lied to Appellant about the "situation." All of this was before the members. The military judge did not abuse his discretion; he provided Appellant what he was due under the Confrontation Clause: an opportunity to impeach the complainant's credibility.

Finally, Appellant argues that Cadet SR's past in- discretion and her lies about it gave her similar motive to lie about her relationship with Appellant.

We de- cline to embrace such a broad, cumulative reading of M.R.E. 412 and its case law. Even according to Appel- lant's own theory, Cadet SR lied about her sexual past to protect herself, not a [449] relationship with another, unlike *United States v. Williams*, 37 M.J. 352 (C.M.A. 1993), or *Olden v. Kentucky*, 488 U.S. 227 (1988). This is not a case like *Collier* in which the appellant asserted she was framed for larceny by her gay lover after the breakup of the relationship. 67 M.J. at 351. Nor does this case involve recent extramarital sex or rejection and invective which might have caused the victim to falsely claim rape, as in *Dorsey*, 16 M.J. at 6. To the ex- tent Appellant might have tried to introduce some non- sexual aspects of his theory of bias via M.R.E. 608(c), he failed to frame or raise this issue as such at trial.

VI.

The decision of the United States Coast Guard Court of Criminal Appeals is affirmed.

BAKER, Judge (concurring in the result):

I concur in the result. In my view, this case is gov- erned by *United States v. Banker*, 60 M.J. 216, 225 (C.A.A.F. 2004). In *Banker*, we concluded that in the context of Military Rule of Evidence (M.R.E.) 412, it is "within the judge's discretion to determine that such a cursory argument [does] not sufficiently articulate how the testimony reasonably established a motive to fabri- cate.... [It is] within the discretion of the military judge to conclude that the offered testimony was not relevant." *Id.* at 225. The burden is on the appellant to prove why the M.R.E. 412 prohibition should be lifted. *Id.*

Appellant's theory of admission was that SR, hav- ing lied to Appellant about her prior sexual misconduct with an enlisted member of the Coast Guard, demon- strated a propensity to lie about her sex life generally and in particular to make false allegations to law enforcement authorities to conceal her own sexual mis- conduct. Appellant argues that SR's misconduct also included engaging in consensual sexual activities with Appellant in the Cadet barracks. Therefore, Appellant argues, he had a constitutional right to cross-examine SR about her prior sexual conduct, notwithstanding the general prohibition on such examination enshrined in M.R.E. 412.

The problem for Appellant is that his theory of ad- mission is too far-fetched to pass constitutional and M.R.E. 403 muster. First, SR had no obligation to tell Appellant about her sexual life and misconduct. It does not logically follow that someone who would lie to pro- tect her privacy from a probing acquaintance would lie to the police and commit perjury. Second, it was SR herself who reported her sexual contact with Appel- lant; this cuts against Appellant's theory that SR would lie to conceal her own misconduct. Third, to support this theory of admission the members needed to know that SR had "lied" to Appellant about her sexual mis- conduct; they did not need to know the details of the prior sexual conduct. This much the military judge permitted.

In my view, Appellant might have a different ap- pellate case if he had argued to this Court that mem- bers needed to know the nature of "the secret" in order to assess beyond a reasonable doubt whether SR might succumb to pressure to protect the secret. This alter- native theory was not the basis of Appellant's appeal before this Court. In any event, it should be noted that the military judge rejected this theory at trial, his con- clusions of law stating:

> While the importance of her secret would be relevant in this fashion, I do not think that the

members would need to know the specifics. At the Article 39(a) session, the Government of- fered a generic formulation that would impress upon the members the seriousness of the se- cret. In essence, the members could be in- formed that the secret was information that if revealed could have an adverse impact on her Coast Guard career, including possibly discipli- nary action under the UCMJ.

Reasonable judges might disagree on whether ad- ditional detail about "the secret" was needed for mem- bers to fairly assess whether this Coast Guard cadet was coerced into sexual conduct to safeguard that se- cret. But **I** am not persuaded that it was plain error. The military judge informed the members that the se- cret exposed the witness to criminal liability and vio- lated academy regulations. This is the very sort of bal- ancing military judges are supposed to conduct [450] when they weigh an accused's rights and a victim's pri- vacy under M.R.E. 412.

ERDMANN, Judge, with whom EFFRON, Chief

Judge, joins (concurring in part and dissenting in

part):

While **I** concur with the majority opinion as to the jurisdictional issue raised by the Government, **I** re- spectfully dissent from the majority's conclusion as to the granted issue. **In** a case where credibility of the complainant was fundamental, the military judge pre- vented the defense from presenting to the panel an ex- planation of the circumstances that would have pro- vided a motive for the complainant to make a false alle- gation of rape.

Background

Cadet Webster Smith was initially charged with twenty-two specifications, the majority of which re- lated to his sexual relationships with female cadets at the United States Coast Guard Academy.

Eleven of those charges were dismissed before trial. At a general court-martial composed of members, Smith was found not guilty of six of the remaining charges. Contrary to his pleas, the members found him guilty of absence without leave, attempted failure to obey a lawful order, sodomy, extortion, and indecent assault. The sodomy, extortion, and indecent assault charges arose out of al- legations made by SR, a female cadet.

In this appeal, Smith asserts that the military judge erred by preventing him from fully cross- examining SR as to her motive and credibility in viola- tion of his Sixth Amendment right to confrontation and the "constitutionally required" exception to Military Rule of Evidence (M.R.E.) 412. M.R.E. 412(b)(1)(C). At trial the defense filed a motion pursuant to M.R.E. 412 requesting permission to cross-examine SR about her alleged statements to Smith concerning a prior sexual encounter she had with an enlisted servicemem- ber. The factual basis for the motion was summarized by the military judge in his findings of fact:

> During the summer training program at the start of their first class year, Cadet Smith and [SR] were both assigned to patrol boats that moored at Station Little Creek.
> Both lived in barracks rooms at the Station. In May 2005, Cadet Smith approached [SR] to inform her that he was hearing rumors from the
> enlisted personnel assigned to the Station that she had a sexual encounter with an enlisted

member assigned to the Station. [SR] told him that this was true, but that it was not a consen- sual encounter. Cadet Smith then informed the enlisted personnel who were spreading the ru- mors that the conduct was not consensual.

On or about 19 October 2005, Cadet Smith again approached [SR]. He told her that he had remained in contact with some of the enlisted personnel assigned to Station Little Creek and that the rumors surrounding her sexual en- counter with the enlisted man had continued. This time she told him that the incident with the enlisted man had been a consensual encoun- ter and that the scope of the encounter had been greater than she had previously de- scribed.

At the Article 32 hearing, [SR] merely stated that she had confided a secret to Cadet Smith. In her 15 February 2006 statement, she merely stated that a situation occurred which led to rumors. On both occasions, she went on to state that on October 19th, she was con- cerned enough that Cadet Smith would expose this secret that she agreed to pose for a picture with him in which both of them were nude, and later that night allowed him to perform cunni- lingus on her then she performed fellatio on him.

In the defense motion, Smith argued that the evi- dence was constitutionally required because "[t]he fact that the alleged victim lied to Cadet Smith about her sexual activity and has misled CGIS about that activity tends to show the alleged victim as untruthful about her sexual conduct generally and specifically has motive to lie about the specific sexual rumors underlying the charge—the very issue before the trier of fact."

The Government opposed the admission of the evi- dence arguing that the substance of SR's secret was not relevant, material, or vital to Smith's defense. In deny- ing the motion the military judge concluded that: [451] while the evidence was relevant, the members did not need to know the specifics, but could be provided with a non-specific summary;[1] although the evidence could show that SR had a propensity to bring false accusa- tions against men with whom she had consensual sexual encounters, the evidence was not strong since the source of the allegation, Smith, was biased; there was a significant difference between SR making a false alle- gation to Smith and making a false allegation to law en- forcement authorities; and the probative value of the evidence was outweighed by the danger of unfair prejudice.

The United States Coast Guard Court of Criminal Appeals affirmed the findings and sentence.

United States v. Smith, 66 M.J. 556, 563 (C.G. Ct. Crim. App. 2008). We review a military judge's decision to admit or exclude evidence for an abuse of discretion. *United States v. Ayala,* 43 M.J. 296, 298 (C.A.A.F. 1995). In doing so, we review findings of fact under the clearly erroneous standard and conclusions of law under the de novo standard. *Id.*

---

[1] The military judge found that "the members could be in- formed that the secret was information that if revealed could have an adverse impact on [SR's] Coast Guard career, including possi- bly disciplinary action under the UCMJ."

Discussion

The evidence at issue was proffered to attack SR's credibility by establishing that she had earlier made a false allegation of a nonconsensual sexual encounter to protect her Coast Guard career. Before addressing the M.R.E. 412 issue, it is worth noting that there is some question as to whether M.R.E. 412 even applies to this type of evidence. The Drafters' Analysis to M.R.E. 412 states "[e]vidence of past false complaints of sexual of- fenses by an alleged victim of a sexual offense is not within the scope of this Rule and is not objectionable when otherwise admissible." *Manual for Courts- Martial, United States*, Analysis of the Military Rules of Evidence app. 22 at A22-36 (2008 ed.).[2] However, given the posture of this case on appeal, and assuming that M.R.E. 412 does apply, the evidence is clearly admissible under the M.R.E. 412 analysis.

1. *Objections Under M.R.E. 412*

"[A] criminal defendant states a violation of the Confrontation Clause by showing that he was prohib- ited from engaging in otherwise appropriate cross- examination designed to show a prototypical form of bias on the part of the witness, and thereby 'to expose to the jury the facts from which jurors ... could appro- priately draw inferences relating to the reliability of the witness.' " *Delaware v. Van Arsdall*, 475 U.S. 673, 680 (1986) (citing *Davis v. Alaska*, 415 U.S. 308, 318 (1974)). "[E]xposure of a witness' motivation in testify-

---

[2] *See also* Fed. R. Evid. 412 advisory committee's note on pro- posed 1994 amendment ("Evidence offered to prove allegedly false prior claims by the victim is not barred by Rule 412. However, the evidence is subject to the requirements of Rule 404.").

ing is a proper and important function of the constitu- tionally protected right of cross-examination." *Id.* At 678-79. "The question is whether '[a] reasonable jury might have received a significantly different impression of [the witness's] credibility had [defense counsel] been permitted to pursue his proposed line of cross-examination.'" *United States v. Collier*, 67 M.J. 347, 352 (C.A.A.F. 2009) (brackets in original) (quoting *Van Arsdall*, 475 U.S. at 680).

"M.R.E. 412 was intended to protect victims of sex- ual offenses from the degrading and embarrassing dis- closure of intimate details of their private lives while preserving the constitutional rights of the accused to present a defense." *United States v. Banker*, 60 M.J. 216, 219 (C.A.A.F 2004). There are, however, three ex- ceptions to the exclusionary provisions of M.R.E. 412.

Smith relied on the third exception that requires the admission of evidence "the exclusion of which would violate the constitutional rights of the accused." M.R.E. 412(b)(1)(C). "This exception addresses an ac- cused's *Sixth Amendment* right of confrontation and *Fifth Amendment* right to a fair trial." *Banker*, 60 M.J. at 221 (citations omitted) (emphasis added). *Banker* requires that "where evidence [452] is offered pursuant to this exception, it is important for defense counsel to detail an accused's theory of relevance and constitu-tional necessity." 60 M.J. at 221. Smith's counsel did just that in this case.

2. *Relevance and Materiality*

In order to properly determine whether evidence is admissible under the constitutionally required excep- tion the military judge must evaluate whether the prof- fered evidence is relevant, material, and favorable to the defense. *Id.* at 222. "[T]he relevancy portion of this test is the same as that employed for the other two ex- ceptions of the rule," which is that "[e]vidence is rele- vant if it has 'any tendency to make the existence of any fact ... more probable or less probable than it would be without the evidence.' M.R.E. 401." *Id.* At 222. The proffered evidence could have impacted SR's credibility by allowing the defense to provide a com- monsense explanation for SR to give false testimony.

That is, when SR learned of the investigation of Smith for alleged sexual offenses, she became concerned that the investigation would produce allegations that she had engaged in prohibited sexual activity[3] with Smith in their dormitory at the Coast Guard Academy, thereby jeopardizing her own career. Thus, she fabri- cated the charges against Smith to protect her career, as she had in the past for the same reason. The military judge found that the evidence would be relevant and **I** agree.

Having found the evidence relevant, the next step for the military judge was to determine whether the evidence was "material and favorable to the accused's defense, and thus whether it is 'necessary'" *Id.* at 222 (citing *United States v. Williams*, 37 M.J. 352, 361 (C.M.A. 1993)).

> In determining whether evidence is material, the military judge looks at "the importance of the issue for which the evidence was offered in relation to the other issues in this case; the ex- tent to which this issue is in dispute; and the

---

[3] Pursuant to Regulations for the Code of Cadets 4-5-05.a.3, sexual conduct is prohibited on Coast Guard Academy installations even if it is between consenting cadets. Cadets found guilty of con- sensual sexual misconduct can be disenrolled. *Id.* at 4-5-05.a.4.

nature of the other evidence in the case pertaining to this issue."

Id. (quoting *United States v. Colon-Angueira*, 16 M.J. 20, 26 (C.M.A. 1983)).

There can be no dispute that testing the credibility of a witness through cross-examination is crucial to the right of confrontation.

> A more particular attack on the witness' credi- bility is effected by means of cross-examination directed toward revealing possible biases, prejudices, or ulterior motives of the witness as they may relate directly to issues or personali- ties in the case at hand. The partiality of a wit- ness is subject to exploration at trial, and is "always relevant as discrediting the witness and affecting the weight of his testimony." 3A J. Wigmore, Evidence § 940, p. 775 (Chadbourn rev. 1970). We have recognized that the expo- sure of a witness' motivation in testifying is a proper and important function of the constitu- tionally protected right of cross-examination.

Davis v. Alaska, 415 U.S. 308, 316 (1974) (citation omit- ted).

> As in *United States v. Dorsey*, 16 M.J. 1, 7 (C.M.A. 1983), this was a "he said-she said" case and for the charges at issue in this appeal,[4] the critical question for the members was the credibility of the sole prosecution witness. Evidence of a motive to fabricate and that SR had alleged that an earlier consensual sexual encounter was nonconsensual in an attempt to protect her career

---

[4] Sodomy, extortion, and indecent assault.

bears directly on SR's credibility as to the allegations she made against Smith. It may have shown that SR had a propensity to lie about consensual sexual encoun- ters when her career was on the line. The materiality of this evidence is not the "lurid nuances of the victim's sexual past" as noted by the majority, but rather the allegation that SR had previously lied about a sexual encounter under similar circumstances. [453]

3.   *Balancing*

Once the military judge has determined that the proffered evidence is relevant and material, the mili- tary judge must undertake the M.R.E. 412 balancing test to determine if the evidence is favorable to the ac- cused's defense.[5] *Banker,* 60 M.J. at 222. The term fa- vorable is synonymous with vital. *Id.* "[W]hen balanc- ing the probative value of the evidence against the danger of unfair prejudice under M.R.E. 412, the mili- tary judge must consider ... factors such as confusion of the issues, misleading the members, undue delay, waste of time, needless presentation of cumulative evidence, [and] also prejudice to the victim's legitimate privacy

---

[5] Commentators have noted that the "constitutionally re- quired" exception may be unnecessary since once it is established that the evidence is constitutionally required, there can be no fur- ther limitation on its admission. *See* 1 Stephen A. Saltzburg et al., *Military Rules of Evidence Manual* § 412.02[4], at 4-194 (6th ed. 2006) ("Any limitation on a constitutional right would be disre- garded whether or not such a Rule existed."); Christopher B. Mueller & Laird C. Kirkpatrick, *Federal Evidence* § 4:81, at 306 (3d ed. 2007) ("The exception is arguably unnecessary because Fed. R. Evid. 412 is subordinate to the Constitution anyway, but perhaps including it diminishes the sense of conflict between the two legal standards.").

interests." *Id.* at 223. The M.R.E. 412 balancing test weighs in Smith's favor. Under the circumstances of this case, any risk of confusion of the issues, misleading the members, wasting time, or presenting cumulative evidence was minimal and is outweighed by the high probative value of this evidence.

In *Dorsey* the court found evidence favorable when it "undermined the credibility of the sole prosecution witness who directly testified to appellant's guilt of the charged offense." *Dorsey,* 16 M.J. at 7. In a similar fashion, admission of a prior false allegation of a non- consensual sexual encounter could have undermined the credibility of SR, the only witness who testified against Smith on the extortion, sodomy, and indecent assault charges.

While the evidence of SR's earlier allegation of a false nonconsensual sexual encounter and her subse- quent admission that the encounter was consensual would have impacted her privacy interests, withholding this constitutionally required evidence from the panel deprived Smith of his best opportunity to provide a mo- tive for SR's allegations and to challenge her credibil- ity. The fact that the military judge allowed the panel to hear that SR had a secret that, if revealed could have an adverse impact on her Coast Guard career, including possibly disciplinary action under the UCMJ, was sim- ply not sufficient. With this limited information about SR's secret, the members were left to speculate whether the secret was a minor disciplinary infraction or a more serious charge, but they had no idea that the proffered evidence directly implicated SR's motive and credibility.[6]

In *Collier* this court found the military judge erred in limiting cross-examination of the complaining wit- ness for possible bias. *Collier*, 67 M.J. at 349. There, the defendant attempted to establish bias by present- ing evidence of the existence of a romantic relationship that ended badly between the accused and the com- plaining witness. *Id.* at 351. The military judge only allowed cross-examination as to the "breakup of a friendship." *Id.* at 351-52. This court found that there was a qualitative difference between the two situations and if the members had been shown evidence of the romantic relationship they might have had a signifi- cantly different impression of the accusing witness' credibility. *Id.* at 352, 353. Similarly, there is a qualita- tive difference between an undisclosed situation that "could have had an adverse impact on [SR's] Coast Guard career" and an allegation that SR had previously made a false allegation of a nonconsensual sexual en- counter to protect her career.

[454] While the military judge found that the evi- dence was not strong because it came from Smith, who had an obvious bias, it is well established that "[t]he weight and credibility of the ... witness are matters for

---

[6] Trial counsel illustrated the range of incidents that the members could have speculated on when, at one point during his argument on the motion, he stated that while the existence of the secret was extremely relevant, the content of the secret was not. Trial counsel argued, "[t]he extortion charge is that there was a secret. It doesn't matter if that secret was whether she liked Smarties. It doesn't matter if she had committed some other fel- ony ...."

the members alone to decide." *United States v. Moss*, 63 M.J. 233, 239 (C.A.A.F. 2006) (citing *United States v. Bins*, 43 M.J. 79, 85 (C.A.A.F. 1995)). The court in *Banker* noted that the role of the military judge is to assure that the evidence meets the usual evidentiary standards. *Banker*, 60 M.J. at 224 (citing *United States v. Platero*, 72 F.3d 806, 812 (10th Cir. 1995)). The court in *Platero* went on to say, "when the Judge decides whether or not a defense is true or false and decides that on the basis of the credibility of the witnesses, the Judge is doing what the jury is supposed to do in a serious criminal case covered by the Sixth Amendment." *Platero*, 72 F.3d at 812.

Smith had a commonsense explanation for SR's claim that the sexual activity was nonconsensual and the military judge's ruling prevented the members from considering this theory. The alleged false accusation was close in time to the allegation made against Smith, both allegations involved military members and both situations presented a motive for SR to lie about the consensual nature of her sexual activities to protect her career. Putting aside the fact that M.R.E. 412 may not even apply to this type of evidence, I would conclude that the evidence should have been admitted under M.R.E. 412. I would further find that the error was not harmless beyond a reasonable doubt as it essentially deprived Smith of his best defense and "the excluded evidence may have tipped the credibility balance in [Smith's] favor." *Moss*, 63 M.J. at 239.

I would reverse the decision of the United States Coast Guard Court of Criminal Appeals and set aside the findings and sentence for Additional Charge I, Specification 1 of Additional Charge II, and Additional Charge III, and remand the case for further proceedings, if any.

Appendix 9

Decision of United States Coast Guard Court of Criminal Appeals, <u>With Appendixes</u>

UNITED STATES COAST GUARD COURT OF CRIMINAL APPEALS

Docket No. 1275

CGCMG 0224

UNITED STATES,

v.

WEBSTER M. SMITH, CADET (E1C), U.S. COAST GUARD,

Decided: 9 April 2008

[66 M.J. 556*]

* * *

[557]

BEFORE MCCLELLAND, TUCHER &
LODGE, Appellate Military Judges

MCCLELLAND, Judge:

Appellant was tried by general court-martial com- posed of members. Contrary to his pleas, Appellant was convicted of one specification of unauthorized absence, in _____

[* Petitioner notes that the opinion that appears in the official reporter includes several redactions. The unredacted version re- printed here was sealed by the court of criminal appeals but un- sealed, by order dated October 29, 2009, by the court of appeals. Also, footnotes 1-6 in the court's opinion, regarding counsel repre- senting the parties, have been omitted.]

violation of Article 86, Uniform Code of Military Justice (UCMJ); one specification of attempted failure to obey a lawful order, in violation of Article 80, UCMJ; one speci- fication of sodomy, in violation of Article 125, UCMJ; one specification of extortion, in violation of Article 127, UCMJ; and one specification of indecent assault, in viola- tion of Article 134, UCMJ. The court sentenced Appel- lant to a dismissal, confinement for six months, and for- feiture of all pay and allowances. The Convening Au- thority approved the sentence as adjudged.

Before this Court, Appellant has assigned six er- rors:

I. The convictions for extortion, sodomy, and indecent assault must be reversed because the military judge violated Appellant's constitutional right to confront his accusers by limiting his cross-examination of SR.

II. If the findings for extortion and indecent assault are set aside, then the sodomy conviction, which is based on private consensual non-commercial activ- ity between adults of equal rank, is unconstitu- tional.

III. The extortion conviction must be overturned be- cause the Government failed to prove that Appel- lant threatened SR with the intent to obtain sexual favors.

IV. The conviction for going from an appointed place of duty cannot stand because the Government failed to prove that Appellant knew that his duty assign- ment required him to remain in Chase Hall after 2200.

V. The evidence was factually insufficient to sustain the conviction for attempted violation of an order.

VI. The Convening Authority erred in summarily de- nying Appellant's request to defer confinement.

We summarily reject the third and fourth assigned errors. The evidence, though circumstantial, is suffi- cient to support the convictions. We will discuss the other assigned errors. We find no error and affirm.

I

Appellant asserts that the military judge erred in limiting his cross-examination of the complaining wit- ness concerning the extortion, sodomy, and indecent assault specifications of which he was found guilty. We will review the military judge's decision *de novo*.[7] [558] If error is found, we will reverse unless we find the er- ror harmless beyond a reasonable doubt.

In May 2005, during the Coast Guard Academy's summer program, Appellant, a Coast Guard Academy cadet, and SR, a female Academy classmate, were as- signed to neighboring cutters in Norfolk, Virginia. Ap- pellant communicated with SR, letting her know that he was hearing rumors about her. They discussed the

---

[7] The Court of Appeals for the Armed Forces has stated that it employs an abuse-of-discretion standard when reviewing claims that a military judge's evidentiary ruling violated the Sixth Amendment right of confrontation. *United States v. Moss*, 63 M.J. 233, 236 (C.A.A.F. 2006); *United States v. Israel*, 60 M.J. 485, 488 (C.A.A.F. 2005). These cases, as well as others preceding them, found error in the trial court's ruling, weakening the claim that they represent holdings as to the standard of review to be applied. In any event, we choose to review this issue *de novo* under our Article 66, UCMJ, responsibility to determine whether the find- ings and sentence, on the basis of the entire record, should be ap- proved. *See United States v. Olean*, 56 M.J. 594, 598-99 (C.G.Ct.Crim.App. 2001).

rumors, and SR told Appellant the story underlying the rumors. (R. at 878, 1320.) SR testified that she told Appellant a part of but not the whole situation; she lied to him by omitting details that would have painted her in a bad light. (R. at 878, 901-02.) Appellant assured her that he would counteract the rumors. (R. at 878,1320.)

On 19 October 2005, Appellant communicated with SR to the effect that the rumors were still being talked about. Again they discussed the rumors, and this time SR told Appellant the complete story of what had hap- pened. (R. at 880, 921, 1321.) Appellant testified to the effect that his source had indicated the story was dif- ferent from what she had originally told him, and that when she told him the complete story, it was indeed "pretty substantially different." (R. at 1321.) SR testi- fied that, at that point, she thought if she did not tell him the whole story, he would stop helping her. (R. at 922.) Her actions in the complete story, she admitted, violated cadet regulations and possibly the UCMJ, but she understood at the time of trial that she would not be prosecuted for them. (R. at 899.) Once she told Ap- pellant the whole story, she testified, he responded that he needed motivation to continue helping her. (R. at 880-81.) Later that evening, Appellant and SR engaged in sexual conduct that became the subject of the extor- tion, indecent assault, and sodomy charges against Ap- pellant. (R. at 881-92.) SR maintained that the reason she engaged in the conduct was because she "was scared to upset him because he had a big secret of mine." (R. at 891.)

Early in the trial, a closed Article 39(a) session was held pursuant to Military Rule of Evidence (M.R.E.) 412 to address the details of the story underlying the rumors, on which the defense proposed to cross-examine SR. According to Appellant, SR's story in May was that she had had a sexual encounter involving oral sex with an enlisted Coast Guard member, that it was not consensual, and that she felt guilty about it be- cause it was not with her boyfriend. (R. at 101-02.) SR's story in October, according to Appellant, was that the sexual encounter was in fact consensual and that it included intercourse as well as oral sex. (R. at 102.) The military judge ruled that SR could be cross- examined concerning the lie in May, but that the de- tails, as described in this paragraph, were not to be brought out.[8]

Appellant contends that the military judge's ruling was a "flagrant violation" of Appellant's Sixth Amend- ment right of confrontation. In defense of the extor- tion, indecent assault, and sodomy charges, Appellant sought to convince the court members that SR was ly- ing about her sexual encounter with Appellant, in par- ticular falsely contending that it was not consensual, and that she was doing so to protect herself from disci- pline. This argument, he asserts, would have been much more persuasive had the members known that before 19 October, SR had been lying to Appellant

---

[8] It is undisputed that the details fall within Military Rule of Evidence (M.R.E.) 412's exclusion. Moreover, SR, a newly- commissioned Coast Guard officer at the time of trial, testified that she was still concerned about the story because "I'm afraid of ru- mors when I go from unit to unit." (R. at 877.) It is for this reason that we continue to treat the details as specified in M.R.E. 412(c), keeping them nonpublic, although M.R.E. 412 addresses itself to admission of evidence, implying that it applies at trials, and does not mention appellate proceedings. Portions of the briefs were sealed, and we held a closed hearing for oral argument on this as- signment of error. We seal portions of this opinion in the same spirit; likewise the dissent.

about her sexual encounter with an enlisted man, in particular falsely contending that it was not consensual, and doing so to protect herself from discipline.

M.R.E. 412 renders evidence inadmissible that is offered to prove a complainant engaged in sexual be- havior other than that involved in the alleged offense. M.R.E. 412(a)(1). However, it excepts, among other things, "evidence the exclusion of which would violate the constitutional rights of the [559] accused." M.R.E. 412(b)(1)(C). An accused has the right to admission of such evidence if it is relevant, material, and favorable to his defense. *United States v. Dorsey*, 16 M.J. 1, 5 (C.M.A. 1983) (citing *United States v. Valenzuela- Bernal*, 458 U.S. 858 (1982)). "Favorable" is further in- terpreted as "vital." *United States v. Banker*, 60 M.J. 216, 222 (C.A.A.F. 2004).

Appellant was properly allowed to cross-examine SR concerning her May 2005 lie, pursuant to M.R.E. 608(b) and the Sixth Amendment. However, the right to confrontation is not absolute. "[T]rial judges retain wide latitude insofar as the Confrontation Clause is concerned to impose reasonable limits on such cross- examination based on concerns about, among other things, harassment, prejudice, confusion of the issues, the witness' safety, or interrogation that is repetitive or only marginally relevant. And as we observed earlier this Term, 'the Confrontation Clause guarantees an *opportunity* for effective cross-examination, not cross- examination that is effective in whatever way, and to whatever extent, the defense might wish.' " *Delaware v. Van Arsdall*, 475 U.S. 673, 679 (1986) (citation omitted). The trial judge could properly restrict Appellant's cross-examination of SR on the basis of M.R.E. 412, ex- cluding, as he did, the details of the May incident,

Dorsey, 16 M.J. at 5; *Banker,* 60 M.J. at 222.

Appellant cites *United States v. Bahr,* 33 M.J. 228 (C.M.A. 1991), and *United States v. Moss,* 63 M.J. 233 (C.A.A.F. 2006), in support of his argument that the de- tails of the May incident were constitutionally required to be admitted. In each of these cases, evidence of a complainant's motive to fabricate was proffered but ex- cluded.[9] In both cases, the court held the exclusion was prejudicial error.

In *Bahr,* the accused was charged with sexual of- fenses against his 14-year-old daughter. The defense offered the daughter's diary, in which she expressed intense dislike of her mother, and proposed to cross- examine her on it to show that she hated her mother. The Court of Military Appeals agreed that this tended to show a motive to testify falsely against her father in order to hurt her mother. Admission of such evidence was required under M.R.E. 608(c) and the Sixth Amendment. 33 M.J. at 233. The defense further sought to cross-examine the child concerning prior false statements to her classmates about being raped by sol- diers in Spain, which she had admitted to counsel were lies she had uttered to attract attention. Again, the court agreed that this line of cross-examination was admissible to show the prosecutrix had a second motive to testify falsely. *Id.* at 233-34.

The accused in *Moss* was charged with sexual of- fenses against his 14-year-old niece. The defense sought to show that the niece fabricated the allegations so as to cast herself as a victim to gain favorable treat-

---

[9] M.R.E. 412 was not implicated in these cases.

from her parents, by cross-examining her and her mother on her acts of misbehavior and the resulting punishments, and on the improvement in the relation- ship with her parents after she reported the allega- tions. 63 M.J. at 235. In this case, too, CAAF held the proposed cross-examination should have been allowed, citing M.R.E. 608(c) and the Sixth Amendment.[10] *Id.* At 237.

The circumstances of these cases are different from those of our case. The girls' claimed motives to fabri- cate, in order to retaliate against her mother and also to gain attention in the one case, and to divert attention from her own misdeeds in the other, were supported by direct evidence or evi-[560]dence from an earlier paral- lel situation. In our case, the argument as to motiva- tion is being made based on an earlier situation claimed to be parallel, but there is a significant difference be- tween the two situations.

It is clear that SR wanted Appellant's help in sup- pressing rumors concerning the May 2005 incident, and it is fair to argue that avoiding discipline was a factor motivating her to lie to Appellant about the details. The motive for SR to falsify the truth regarding the

---

[10] During the trial of this case, there was little mention of mo- tive as a basis for admission of the disputed evidence. M.R.E. 608(c) was not cited. In the defense's Notice Pursuant to M.R.E. 412, the argument referred to credibility generally, and went on to argue that the evidence at issue "tends to show the alleged victim as untruthful about her sexual conduct generally and specifically has motive to lie about the specific sexual rumors underlying the charge." (Appellate Ex. XIX at 3 (citing *United States v. Dorsey,* 16 M.J. 1 (C.M.A. 1983)).) However, the "motive to lie" point was not developed. In the context of this case, this omission makes no difference to our analysis.

May incident can be directly linked to her concern for either UCMJ or administrative action against her for engaging in consensual sexual relations with an enlisted member. There is no apparent similar motive to fabri- cate her story regarding the events on 19 October 2005. There is no evidence in the record, no suggestion, and no reason to believe that anyone knew about the 19 Oc- tober conduct other than Appellant and SR, and thus no reason to believe a preemptive false report on her part would be useful to her. Since no one else knew about the events that took place in the cadet barracks that night, there was no reason for SR to be concerned with either UCMJ or administrative action against her, and therefore no reason for her to falsify the informa- tion when she made her report[11] or when she testified at trial. Appellant could have cross-examined her upon her motive for making that report, instead of relying solely on a claimed parallel with the May incident, but did not do so. Hence, there is no evidence at all of mo- tive to fabricate, and the earlier situation is not parallel.

The military judge's ruling allowed Appellant to at- tack SR's credibility by means of showing a prior lie. It precluded Appellant from showing that the prior lie pertained to the nature (consensual or not) of a prior sexual encounter with someone else, but did not pre- clude Appellant from attempting to show, by other means, that SR had a motive to lie in her testimony against Appellant. Nor did it preclude Appellant from "portray[ing] the witness as the architect of a scheme

---

[11] SR provided a signed statement dated 15 February 2006 to the Coast Guard Investigative Service containing the allegations against Appellant. (Appellate Ex. XVII, Enclosure 13; Appellate Ex. XXI

of false allegations intended to cover up her own misconduct," as the dissent complains. That the witness lied came into evidence (R. at 901), as did the fact that the lie pertained to her misconduct (R. at 899-901).

We further disagree with the dissent that her tes- timony "created a substantially different impression of her credibility than what the defense had tried to show—namely, that SR had knowingly provided Appel- lant with false information" for the purpose of using him to counter a career-threatening rumor, impliedly by disseminating the false information. She testified on direct examination that she "did not tell [Appellant] the whole situation," but only "[a] little bit of it." (R. at 878.) But she also admitted, under cross-examination, that she had lied to him, that the bits she had omitted painted her in a bad light. (R. at 901-02.) Appellant's testimony reflected that her statements to him had been "substantially different." (R. at 1321.) The mili- tary judge's ruling prevented the members from judg- ing for themselves whether her behavior should be characterized as a lie or something less, but it did not prevent Appellant's defense counsel from arguing, as he did, that she admitted lying.[12] (R. at 1510.)

----

[12] The dissent propounds the theory that SR sought to have Appellant lie for her. Both her testimony and Appellant's testi- mony imply that he volunteered to help her suppress the rumors, without her asking. (R. at 878, 1320.) She also testified that on 19 October, she said to him, "I'm not gonna ask you to lie for me." (R. at 903.) As the dissent notes, there is nothing to indicate just what she hoped for or expected him to do to "squash" or suppress ru- mors. On the evidence, it would be fair argument to say that she sought to have him lie for her, but the defense did not actually make that argument at trial.

145

J As noted above, an accused has the right to admis- sion of evidence despite M.R.E. 412 if it is relevant, ma- terial, and vital to his defense. *United States v. Dorsey*, 16 M.J. 1, 5 (C.M.A. 1983); *United States v. Banker*, 60 M.J. 216, 222 (C.A.A.F. 2004). In this case, we find that the evidence sought to be admitted was no more than superficially relevant, was not material, and was not vital to his [561] defense. We find no error in the mili- tary judge's ruling against Appellant.[13]

II

Appellant asserts that if he prevails on the previ- ous assignment, clearly necessitating reversal of the extortion and indecent assault convictions, the sodomy conviction must also be reversed because it would be unconstitutional under *Lawrence v. Texas*, 539 U.S. 558 (2003).

In *United States v. Marcum*, 60 M.J. 198, 206 (C.A.A.F. 2004), the court held that *Lawrence* applies to the military, but Article 125, the UCMJ's punitive article on sodomy, is not facially unconstitutional. Rather, the court concluded "that its application must be addressed in context," that is, is it constitutional as applied? *Id.* The court set forth three questions to be considered.

---

[13] The military judge did not explicitly find that the evidence was relevant, but did say, "I agree that this theory would be a valid reason for admitting this evidence under M.R.E. 412(b)(1)(C)." (Appellate Ex. CLIII at 3.) He went on to find that "the minimal probative value of this evidence is outweighed by danger of unfair prejudice to [SR]'s privacy interests [per M.R.E. 412(c)(3)] and the potential danger of sidetracking the [members'] attention to a collateral issue [per M.R.E. 403]." *Id.*

First, was the conduct that the accused was found guilty of committing of a nature to bring it within the liberty interest identified by the Supreme Court? Second, did the conduct en- compass any behavior or factors identified by the Supreme Court as outside the analysis in *Lawrence*? Third, are there additional factors relevant solely in the military environment that affect the nature and reach of the *Lawrence* liberty interest?

Id. at 206-07 (citation omitted).

In the absence of the coercive element of extortion, Appellant's conduct might be characterized as private, consensual sexual activity between adults. We may as- sume, as the court did in *Marcum*, that the conduct would be within the *Lawrence* liberty interest. Since Appellant and SR were both first-class cadets and not in the same chain of command, unlike the situation in *Marcum*, we may also assume that the conduct would not encompass behavior or factors identified as being outside the *Lawrence* analysis. However, in the lan- guage of *United States v. Stirewalt*, 60 M.J. 297, 304 (C.A.A.F. 2004), Appellant's conduct "squarely impli- cates the third prong of the framework."

The Regulations for the Corps of Cadets includes an Article 4-5-05 entitled Sexual Misconduct. (Appel- late **Ex. XXIV.**) Paragraph a.3 thereof prohibits sexual conduct on board military installations, which includes the Academy, even if between consenting cadets. We find that Appellant's conduct, as he testified to it (R. at 1326-27), was outside any protected liberty interest recognized in *Lawrence. See Stirewalt*, 60 M.J. at 304 (liberty interest is considered "in light of the estab-

lished ... regulations and the clear military interests of

147

discipline and order that they reflect"). We note that a holding otherwise would apparently yield the anomalous result that the regulation would be enforceable as to all forms of sexual conduct except sodomy, as the Government pointed out at oral argument.[14]

The presence of the regulation readily distin- guishes this case from those of the Army Court of Criminal Appeals opinions attached to Appellant's brief, in which in-barracks consensual sodomy convic- tions were overturned. In one of them, the opinion specifies that there was no evidence of a barracks pol- icy prohibiting the conduct. *United States v. Meno*, ARMY 20000733, at 4 (A.Ct.Crim.App. Jun. 22, 2005) (per curiam). In the other, a guilty plea case, the ac- cused had not admitted any facts that would take the case out of the *Lawrence* liberty interest.[15] *United States v. Bullock*, ARMY 20030534, at 5 (A.Ct.Crim.App. Nov. 30, [562] 2004).

We are not aware of any court-martial appellate decision overturn- ing a sodomy conviction based on *Lawrence* when there was a regulation aside from Article 125, UCMJ, prohib- iting the behavior.[16]

---

[14] We have found no authority suggesting that military regu- lation of sexual conduct generally may be unconstitutional.

[15] Appellant's clemency request to the Convening Authority, dated 22 August 2006, attached another Army Court of Criminal Appeals opinion and cited a Navy Court of Criminal Appeals opin- ion, each of which involved a guilty plea with no indication or ad- mission by the accused of additional factors taking the case out of the *Lawrence* liberty interest.

[16] Under the circumstances of this case, even if Appellant were found not guilty of extortion and even if there were no regu-

Appellant was charged with violating an order prohibiting him from contact with cadets.   He was con- victed of an attempt to violate the order. He contends that the evidence was factually insufficient to support the conviction, in that his attempt to contact a cadet took place the day before the order was issued.

The specification charges violation of a paragraph of a written order issued by the Commandant of Cadets on 7 December 2005, which is Prosecution Exhibit 4. It is styled as an amendment to a written order he had issued on 5 December 2005, which is Defense Exhibit F.[17]   The Commandant of Cadets issued the written or- der of 5 December at the time Appellant was removed from the barracks.   (R. at 820, 1351.) Appellant's ac- knowledgment of receipt is recorded on Defense Ex- hibit F at 0410 on "5 DEC 05." The Commandant of Cadets issued the written order of 7 December after receiving legal advice (R. at 820), but the intent of the order had not changed   (R.   at 807). Appellant's   ac- knowledgment of receipt is recorded on Prosecution Exhibit 4 at 1600 on "DEC 05" (sic). This order was is- sued after the Commandant of Cadets had referred al- legations of sexual assault against Appellant to Coast

lation, it is not clear that the conduct would be within the *Law- rence* liberty interest. We do not reach that question.

[17]   Defense Exhibit F was admitted (R. at 818), although it is not listed in the index as an exhibit admitted into evidence and is found in the record with exhibits that were not admitted. Appellant was charged with violating an order pro- hibiting him from contact with cadets. He was con- victed of an attempt to violate the order. He contends that the evidence was factually insufficient to support the conviction, in that his attempt to contact a cadet took place the day before the order was issued.

Guard Investigative Service (CGIS) for investigation.[18] (R at 814.)

The order of 7 December alleged to have been violated reads, "You are prohibited from any contact of any kind, directly or indirectly, through any source, or by any means, with Coast Guard Academy Cadets wherever they are located; to include text messages, emails, or phone calls." (Prosecution Ex. 4.) This dif-fers from the order of 5 December by the added words, "directly or indirectly, though any source, or by any means," and "wherever they are located."

The specification alleges violation of the order by, "on or about 16 December 2005, ... wrongfully sending an instant message to [KS], with the intention of having [KS] contact Cadet [KN, an Academy classmate of Ap-pellant]."

KS and KN were close friends. (R. at 408, 423, 496, 555; Defense Ex. A.) KS testified that she received an instant message from Appellant in December 2005. (R. at 519.) The text of the instant message is found in Prosecution Exhibit 1 without any marker as to date of origin, and includes the words, "I need you to make sure that she knows that I hope that everything is physically and emotionally ok with her right now." KS understood this to mean Appellant wanted her to relay a message to KN. (R. at 519.) She saved it to her com-puter desktop, intending to relay it to KN, but when she realized that she would be unable to do so before taking a trip, she emailed the text to herself. (R. at 519-20.) Prosecution Exhibit 1 is a printout of the

[18] Appellant was acquitted of several charges growing out of that investigation.

email, dated 16 December 2005. KS testified that she had received the instant message a few—less than ten—days before that. (R. at 560-61.)

Appellant testified that he had sent an instant mes- sage to KS on 6 December 2005 (R. at 1333), before re- ceiving information that he was not supposed to contact any cadets *indirectly* (R. at 1351), but none after re- ceiving the order the next day prohibiting *indirect* con- tact with KN (R. at 1334).

Appellant argues that his testimony was certain as to the date he sent the message and KS's testimony was uncertain, and therefore his version must be ac- cepted. Apparently the members did not believe Ap- pellant's version and believed KS's testimony that she had received the instant message a few (less than ten) days before 16 December. [563] We are satisfied that the evidence supports the finding that Appellant sent the instant message after he received the 7 December order.[19]

IV

Appellant asserts error on the part of the Conven- ing Authority in summarily denying his request for de- ferment of the sentence to confinement.

Shortly after the trial ended at 1856 hours on 28 June 2006, Appellant submitted a written request for a one-week deferment of the sentence of confinement.

---

[19] We reject Appellant's suggestion that the 7 December amendment came about because the Commandant of Cadets learned Appellant had sent the instant message the previous day. (Appellant Br. 35.) There is no evidence and no reason to suspect that anyone other than Appellant and KS knew about the instant message at the time.

The Convening Authority memorialized his action on the request by writing on it, "Request Denied," his sig- nature, and the date, "06/28/06." This was error, as such action must not only be in writing, R.C.M. 1101(c)(3), but also "must include the reasons upon which the action is based." *United States v. Sloan*, 35 M.J. 4, 7 (C.M.A. 1992). The Government concedes the error, but contends that Appellant is not entitled to re-lief. (Government Br. 14-15.)

Appellant claims prejudice in that he was "paraded in front of frenzied members of the media ... in what can only be described as a ... 'perp walk.' "[20] (Appellant Br. 38.) The Government's affidavits contradict Appel- lant's version of events. This Court has extremely lim- ited authority to resolve factual disputes that arise from post-trial submissions. *United States v. Ginn*, 47 M.J. 236, 238 (C.A.A.F. 1997).

Nevertheless, assuming Appellant's version of the facts, we agree with the Government that no relief is due. We find that the Convening Authority's failure to state any reason for denying the deferment request, while error, was harmless. Appellant served the same amount of confinement he would have served if the de- ferment had been granted, albeit without a week of de- lay in its commencement. Assuming he suffered the humiliating and embarrassing experience he describes, we know of no precedent for relief, and we are not in- clined to grant relief. *See United States v. Sloan*, 35 M.J. 4 (C.M.A. 1992); *United States v. Brownd*, 6 M.J.

---

[20] Appellant claims that his affidavit is corroborated by, and the Government's affidavits conflict with, media reports. We de- cline to accept media statements as evidence or take judicial notice of them.

338 (C.M.A. 1979). Distasteful though it may be, we do not believe the criminal law has occasion to take cogni- zance of such an experience. In any event, there is no guarantee that a deferment of confinement would have avoided exposure to the media when he reported for confinement at the end of the deferment.

Decision

We have reviewed the record in accordance with Article 66, UCMJ. Upon such review, the findings and sentence are determined to be correct in law and fact and, on the basis of the entire record, should be ap- proved. Accordingly, the findings of guilty and the sen- tence, as approved below, are affirmed.

Judge   LODGE
concurs.

TUCHER, Judge (concurring in part and dissenting in part):

I concur with the majority decision on Assignments **II, IV, V, and VI   I** dissent from the decision on As- signments **I** and **III.**

I agree with the majority opinion that admission of the underlying details of SR's secret—namely, her prior sexual encounter with an enlisted member—was subject to some limitation under Military Rule of Evi- dence (M.R.E.) 412. I would find, however, that the military judge abused his discretion when he prohibited the defense from cross-examining SR on her false statement to Appellant that the encounter was noncon- sensual, since this evidence was highly probative of the defense theory that SR engaged in a pattern of fabrica- tion to avoid discipline. As discussed below, I believe that the military judge erred when he decided the ad- missibility of this evidence based on his own credibili-

[564]ty determination of the only two witnesses in- volved. The military judge also erred in not consider- ing important factors that favored admission of the de- fense evidence, including that the Government made first use of evidence of SR's secret in its case-in-chief to prove that she was extorted and coerced into sexual relations with Appellant; that SR's credibility was a key element in an otherwise uncorroborated case; and that the strength of the Government's case turned on the members finding the presence of subtle psychologi- cal influences that overcame SR's will. The excessive restrictions imposed on Appellant's Sixth Amendment confrontation rights allowed SR to testify through non- factual euphemisms on critical issues related to the Government's proof and her own credibility, and al- lowed the Government to create a substantially differ- ent impression of her truthfulness than what the de- fense had sought to show through the excluded evi- dence.

It is well-settled that "a primary interest secured by [the confrontation clause of the Sixth Amendment] is the right of cross-examination." *Douglas v. Ala- bama*, 380 U.S. 415, 418 (1965). "Cross-examination is the principal means by which the believability of a wit- ness and the truth of his testimony are tested." *Davis v. Alaska*, 415 U.S. 308, 316 (1974). Moreover, "the ex- posure of a witness' motivation in testifying is a proper and important function of the constitutionally protected right of cross-examination." *Id.* at 316-17. In military courts-martial, the right to attack the partiality of a witness is primarily secured under M.R.E. 608(c), which provides for the admission of evidence that shows bias, prejudice, or any motive to misrepresent through cross-examination of witnesses or extrinsic evidence. *See United States v. Hunter*, 21 M.J. 240, 242

(C.M.A. 1986); *United States v. Saferite*, 59 M.J. 270 (C.A.A.F. 2004).

Although trial judges have broad discretion to im- pose reasonable limits on cross-examination to address concerns over harassment, prejudice, confusion of the issues, the witness' safety, or interrogation that is re- petitive or only marginally relevant, this discretion is not without boundaries. Where the accuracy and truth- fulness of the witness' testimony are "key elements" in the Government's case, a trial court's refusal to allow the defendant to cross-examine the witness regarding possible bias, motive, or prejudice is a violation of his Sixth Amendment rights. *Davis*, 415 U.S. at 317-18; *see also Saferite*, 59 M.J. at 273 ("Evidence of bias can be powerful impeachment."); *United States v. Moss*, 63 M.J. 233, 236 (C.A.A.F. 2006) ("When the military judge excludes evidence of bias, the exclusion raises issues regarding an accused's Sixth Amendment right to con-frontation."); *United States v. Bins*, 43 M.J. 79, 84 (C.A.A.F. 1995) ("When the defense offers this evi- dence, it may deny confrontation rights to exclude it.");
United States v. Foster, 986 F.2d 541, 543 (D.C. Cir. 1993) ("The more important the witness to the govern- ment's case, the more important the defendant's right, derived from the Confrontation Clause of the Sixth Amendment, to cross-examine the witness.").

Evidence that SR had made a prior false claim of sexual assault to Appellant should have been admissi- ble at trial because the central issue was whether SR consented during their sexual encounter on 19 October 2005, and SR was the only Government witness on the issue of consent. The defense should have been able to show that because SR had falsely informed Appellant that her prohibited sexual encounter with an enlisted member was nonconsensual, members could infer that she had followed a similar scheme in fabricating a false complaint of indecent assault against Appellant, where the motive underlying each statement was SR's fear of being disciplined. Here, the record of trial shows that SR relied on Appellant to contain rumors that were cir- culating over what prosecutors cryptically referred to as her "bad situation" or "secret." (R. at 881, 901, 922- 23.) Both SR's "bad situation" and her encounter with Appellant in Chase Hall involved a military nexus that, if disclosed, subjected SR to discipline. Both incidents were connected, in that the encounter in Chase Hall apparently was meant to secure Appellant's continued assistance in "suppressing" rumors regarding the ear-lier encounter.

[565] **I** find it significant that the Government made **first** use of evidence of SR's secret during its case-in-chief. Although the prosecution was able to present evidence that SR was coerced into unwanted sexual relations with Appellant by the implied threat that he would reveal the facts of her "bad situation," the defense was prohibited from showing that this same fear of disclosure weighed so heavily in SR's mind that she relied on Appellant to disseminate false infor- mation concerning her secret. The anomalous result was that the members heard only the Government's evidence on the question of SR's motivation in submit- ting to Appellant's advances, while the defense was un- able to complete the picture by showing the depths of her fear and the lengths she allegedly had gone—and was prepared to go—to shield the facts of her miscon- duct.

I disagree that the cross-examination allowed the defense was adequate to develop SR's motive to testify falsely against Appellant. The sexual encounter be- tween SR and Appellant had many outward appearances of being consensual. The Government's case of indecent assault was not strong and turned on the members finding the existence of coercion that was suf- ficient to overcome the victim's will. Resolving this is- sue necessarily required the members to carefully evaluate the potentially subtle psychological pressure that resulted from Appellant's veiled threat to reveal the truth about SR's secret—a threat that Appellant denied making. Certainly, one explanation for SR's en- counter with Appellant was that she felt coerced into unwanted sexual relations. Another entirely plausible explanation was that the encounter resulted from her own calculation that Appellant needed additional "mo- tivation" to continue spreading false information on her behalf.[1] Both scenarios would account for the consider- able pressure SR was under after Appellant informed her that rumors still were circulating about her secret, but the latter would not necessarily describe extortion or an indecent assault.[2] Appellant could not develop this alternate scenario at trial because he was prohib- ited from adequately addressing SR's prior false state- ment.

In addition, the Government offered no evidence of a fresh complaint and no other evidence to support SR's

---

[1] The defense attempted to develop this alternate theory dur- ing cross-examination of SR, but was hamstrung by its inability to speak directly to the facts of the prior false allegation. (R. at 903.)

[2] In fact, the Government, in apparent acknowledgment of the subtle psychological pressures at work, responsibly determined that it would not charge Appellant with forcible sodomy. In its answer and brief, the Government explained, "[a]s a practical mat- ter, it would be difficult to convict someone of forcible sodomy on these facts, however, that does not mean that the conduct was con- sensual." (Government Br. 7.)

account of the incident involving Appellant.

SR was the Government's key witness against Appellant—in fact, SR's testimony was the only evidence supporting Appellant's conviction on extortion and indecent as- sault. Moreover, her own testimony on the question of consent was far from conclusive. For example, al- though SR testified that at one point during their en- counter she pushed Appellant's head aside and told him, "Please don't," she also testified that they kissed each other and exchanged back massages; that he told her, "You don't have to if you don't want to"; and that she thanked him for his support— presumably in refer- ence to his assistance in defusing rumors regarding her secret. (R. at 885-86, 889-92, 914-17.) On the unusual facts of this case, it was essential that the defense be given wide latitude to explore SR's credibility, and to fully develop any motive reasonably raised by the evi- dence that she would bring a false allegation of sexual assault against Appellant. *See Moss*, 63 M.J. at 236 ("rules of evidence should be read to allow liberal ad- mission of bias-type evidence").

The members eventually did hear SR admit that her secret involved a violation of Cadet Regulations (R. at 899), and that she had misled Appellant about the circumstances, saying, "Yes, **I** did lie to him" (R. at 901). In addition, defense counsel argued in closing that SR "admitted she lied to Cadet Smith." (R. at 1510.) **This** limited impeachment allowed the defense was in- adequate given that a general attack on a witness' credibility is not the same as a showing of bias or mo-tive.

See Davis, 415 U.S. at 316-[566]17.

Here, the members never were able to place SR's admission that she had lied to Appellant in any factual context, be- cause they never heard what the secret was or what she had lied about. The members only heard that SR had lied to Appellant in the past, not why she would have lied in bringing allegations against Appellant.

More importantly, SR was able to minimize her lie to Appellant by testifying that she had only omitted certain details from her account, saying, "I just didn't tell him all that occurred," and also that she told him, "I'm not gonna ask you to lie for me." (R. at 902-03.) Her testimony on this point created a substantially dif- ferent impression of her credibility than what the de- fense had tried to show—namely, that SR had know- ingly provided Appellant with false information, which he then used to counter a career-threatening rumor. *See Olden v. Kentucky*, 488 U.S. 227, 232 (1988) (defendant states a violation of Confrontation Clause if a "reasonable jury might have received a significantly different impression of [the witness'] credibility" had excluded line of cross-examination been allowed). Es- tablishing this point was essential, as the crux of Appel- lant's defense was that SR had followed a pattern of fabrication to avoid discipline that was revealed by like motives from a prior scheme. Given this record, where SR was able to downplay her lie as a mere omission of details, and the defense was not allowed to inform the members what SR had lied about or the lengths she was prepared to go to protect her career, the members may well have concluded that the defense was engaged in a "speculative and baseless line of attack on the credibility of an apparently blameless witness." *Davis*, 415 U.S. at 318.

The military judge issued his ruling under M.R.E. 412, which broadly prohibits the introduction of evi- dence of a victim's past sexual behavior or sexual pre-disposition, unless the evidence fits into one of three narrow exceptions.[3]   Appellant moved to admit the facts of SR's secret under M.R.E. 412(b)(1)(C), which provides an exception for "evidence the exclusion of which would violate the constitutional rights of the ac- cused."[4] Evidence that is offered under an enumerated exception to M.R.E. 412 shall be admitted if the mili- tary judge determines that the evidence is relevant and that the probative value outweighs the danger of unfair prejudice—i.e., prejudice to the privacy interests of the alleged victim. *See* M.R.E. 412(c)(3); *United States v. Sanchez*, 44 M.J. 174, 178 (C.A.A.F. 1996). In addition, relevant evidence that is offered under the constitu- tionally required exception must be admitted if it is ma- terial and favorable to the defense, and therefore is necessary. *United States v. Banker*, 60 M.J. 216, 222 (C.A.A.F. 2004).

---

[3] M.R.E. 412 is modeled after Federal Rule of Evidence 412 and is intended to protect victims of sexual offenses from degrad- ing and embarrassing disclosure of intimate details of their private lives while preserving the constitutional rights of the accused to present a defense. Appendix 22 at A22-36, Manual for Courts- Martial, United States (2005 ed.).

[4] I agree with the majority that the trial defense team did not precisely address the admissibility of the evidence in terms of SR's "motive" to fabricate. Indeed, it appears that the defense objec- tion has assumed greater clarity and focus on appeal. The defense, however, did argue at trial that the evidence implicated Appel- lant's confrontation rights to show the witness's "biases and ... credibility," in that it revealed SR's "pattern" of claiming that pro- hibited consensual relations were coerced when disclosure could be damaging to her career. (R. at 97-98.) By focusing on SR's con- scious decision to lie under similar circumstances in order to avoid punishment, the defense adequately raised the issue of SR's mo- tive to fabricate allegations against Appellant.

In a detailed ruling, the military judge correctly determined that evidence of a prior false claim of sexual assault was relevant evidence of SR's motive to make a false claim of indecent assault against Appellant, stat- ing, "I agree that this theory would be a valid reason for admitting this evidence under M.R.E. 412(b)(1)(C) ...." (Appellate Ex. CLIII at 3.) The military judge reasoned:

> [I]f the members hear that [SR] originally told Cadet Smith that a sexual encounter with an- other man was non-consensual, and then later admitted that it in fact was consensual, then the members could ... infer that the same thing is happening in this case. *Id.*

However, the military judge then went on to con- clude that the evidence had "low" probative value be- cause:

[567] [T]he evidence proffered that [SR] made these statements is not strong since it comes from the accused, who has an obvious bias. [SR]'s written statement and Article 32 testi- mony on this point is not clear. She admitted at the Article 32 that she only partially confided in Cadet Smith in May and fully confided in him on October 19th; however, this is far from proof that she initially claimed that the encounter was non-consensual. In fact, it is consistent with the rest of Cadet Smith's Article 39(a) tes- timony that on October 19th she told him the scope of the sexual encounter had been greater than she had previously described. *Id.*

I would find that the military judge erred when he decided the probative value of motive evidence based on his evaluation of the credibility of the only two wit- nesses involved. It is the members' role to determine whether a witness' testimony is credible or biased. *Bins*, 43 M.J. at 85. "In applying M.R.E. 412, the judge is not asked to determine if the proffered evidence is true; it is for the members to weigh the evidence and determine its veracity." *Banker*, 60 M.J. at 224. Ac- cordingly, relevant and material evidence of a prior false allegation of sexual assault is no less admissible merely because it is offered through the testimony of the criminal accused.

This is particularly so here, where SR—the only other witness to the conversation in issue— secured her unavailability to testify at the motions hearing by invoking her rights against self- incrimination.[5] (R. at 79.) In a credibility contest be- tween Appellant and SR, it should have been up to the members to resolve discrepancies in their respective accounts and decide whom to believe.

As a second basis for excluding the defense evi- dence, the military judge concluded that SR's state-—————————————

---

[5] Because SR refused to testify, the military judge based his findings on Appellant's in-court testimony, SR's prior written statement, and the non-verbatim summary of her Article 32 testi- mony. Based on my review of the complete record, **I** would find that there was at least a reasonable probability that SR provided Appellant with a false account of her secret—namely that the en- counter was non-consensual—which he then used to counter ru- mors on her behalf. Appellant's testimony concerning their initial conversation was partially corroborated in several key respects by SR's trial testimony, including her admission that the conversation took place, that she had "lied" to Appellant by omitting details that presented her in a "bad light," and that Appellant had assisted her by "squashing" rumors of her secret. (R. at 878, 901-02.)

ment to Appellant was materially different from a re- port that she subsequently provided to investigators. The military judge stated:

> [E]ven if [SR] falsely told the accused *in confi- dence* that her sexual encounter with the enlisted man was non-consensual *in an effort to suppress rumors*, this would have little value in proving that her *official* allegations against Cadet Smith *resulting in a public trial* are also false.

(Appellate Ex. **CLIII** at 3.)

The military judge then concluded, "[T]he minimal probative value of this evidence is outweighed by dan- ger of unfair prejudice to [SR's] privacy interests and the potential danger of sidetracking the member's [sic] attention to a collateral issue ...." *Id.*

In a trial on charges of extortion and coerced sex- ual relations, **I** do not agree that the defense intrudes in a collateral matter by making an inquiry into facts that describe the victim's fear that her secret will be re- vealed. Proof of the secret's existence and the genu- ineness of SR's fear of disclosure were key issues in the Government's case against Appellant, and the defense had a right to explore them, subject to carefully tai- lored restrictions respecting SR's privacy.[6] Moreover,

---

[6] The military judge clearly recognized the relevance of the content of the secret to the extortion and indecent assault offenses, observing, "[I]f the secret is about something that is completely inconsequential, it makes it less likely that [SR] would have been willing to do something against her will." (R. at 112.) Ultimately, however, the Government was able to prove both the existence and importance of the secret through the witness's layering on of additional conclusory statements.

163

by focusing on the confidential versus official nature of SR's two statements, the military judge overlooked the greater significance of the defense proffer. The defense theory was that SR's ultimate motive in avoiding disci- pline was revealed in her expectation that Appellant would place his reputation on the line and communicate false information to counter rumors then in circulation about her secret.[7] The defense argued that [568] this same motive was also present in her complaint against Appellant, and it seems an artificial distinction to say that the formality of the complaint process somehow altered SR's overriding concern for protecting her ca- reer. *Compare United States v. Bahr*, 33 M.J. 228, 233 (C.M.A. 1991) (error to exclude evidence of witness' prior false statements to classmates that she had been sexually assaulted; evidence was admissible to show witness' motive to testify falsely against accused in or- der to call attention to herself).

The majority largely sidesteps the problems with the M.R.E. 412 order and under its Article 66(c), Uni- form Code of Military Justice (UCMJ), authority con- cludes that the instant case involves non-parallel statements—an earlier statement to Appellant where avoiding discipline was a factor in SR's motivation to lie, and a second statement to law enforcement investi-

---

[7] There is no dispute that SR did not actively seek out Appel- lant to lie for her concerning her secret. However, after furnishing Appellant with an allegedly false account of her secret, SR appar- ently did nothing to discourage Appellant from using that informa- tion to counter rumors that were in circulation. In fact, SR's ap- proval of Appellant's efforts to "help her" by suppressing rumors was reflected in her own trial testimony (R. at 901, 922-23, 926), and Appellant's threatened withholding of that assistance ulti- mately formed the basis of the Government's extortion charge.

gators where no such motive existed because nobody else knew about the encounter and SR had no reason to fear UCMJ action. The majority emphatically con- cludes that because SR had no possible motive to fabri- cate her allegations against Appellant, the earlier statement was not relevant and therefore was inadmis- sible at trial. The flaw in the majority's argument is the implicit assumption that no circumstances other than the *actual disclosure* of the facts surrounding the Chase Hall encounter could have provided SR with the motive to fabricate allegations of sexual assault. In my view, the timing, content, and circumstances surround- ing SR's initial report to investigators all point to the making of an intrinsically unreliable statement, and provide sufficient grounds to question SR's motives in bringing her allegations against Appellant.

The record reveals that on 5 December 2005, Coast Guard Investigative Service (CGIS) agents inter- viewed Appellant—the other person who knew of the Chase Hall encounter—as part of a large-scale probe into allegations of his sexual misconduct at the Coast Guard Academy. SR was not interviewed by CGIS un- til almost two months later, on 9 February 2006,[8] at which time she discussed her allegations against Appel- lant but specifically refused to address the details of her secret. SR's self-censored initial report reveals that she had made the understandable but nevertheless calculated decision to limit the disclosure of information that could be harmful to her career.[9] Such a decision on

---

[8] The record does not disclose whether SR voluntarily came forward or was first approached by CGIS.

[9] In her signed statement to CGIS dated 15 February 2006, SR also indicated, "A situation occurred, that I do not which [sic]

SR's part following a considerable opportunity for re- flection necessarily calls into question the completeness and reliability of her contemporaneous allegations against Appellant. Given the visibility of this dragnet investigation, the four-month delay between the Chase Hall encounter and SR's initial report, and her selective and continued withholding of facts that did not reflect favorably on her, it certainly was possible that SR fab- ricated or embellished details of her allegation against Appellant as a preemptive strike to avoid discipline, based on *her fear or expectation* that the true facts of their encounter, if not already known by investigators, likely would be discovered.[10] Accord-

[569]ingly, the two statements were "parallel" not because anyone else knew the facts, but because of the illegality of the en- counters and SR's fear that the true facts *could be* dis- covered. Whether or not SR actually formed the mo- tive to fabricate allegations against Appellant was an

---

to discuss, which led to rumors (which were grossly exaggerated)." (Appellate Ex. XVII, Enclosure 13 at 1; Appellate Ex. XXI at 2.) SR's clear attempt to downplay the rumors while at the same time refusing to address them indicates, in my mind at least, a concern for UCMJ or administrative action, if not a desire to deflect official interest in her own behavior.

[10] Given the ongoing CGIS investigation, there certainly would have been risks to SR in not stepping forward at all. SR likely had no way of knowing if Appellant had already reported their encounter to CGIS agents, leaving the possibility of an unre- butted, potentially career-threatening allegation of sexual miscon- duct in the hands of authorities. There also was the risk that Ap- pellant might decide to cooperate with authorities and make a pre- emptive disclosure at a future time. The argument that the record completely foreclosed the possibility of fabrication by SR would make more sense if SR had made a prompt and complete report of her allegations against Appellant at a time prior to the CGIS in- vestigation. That did not happen in this case

issue that that the members should have decided at trial.

Faced with a recalcitrant key witness who refused to testify at the motions hearing, the Government ob- tained a windfall through the erroneous application of M.R.E. 412.

At trial, SR provided conclusory testi- mony regarding her "bad situation" and Appellant's prior role in "squashing" career-threatening rumors, for the purpose of showing that she was coerced into unwanted sexual relations after Appellant impliedly threatened to reveal the truth about her secret.

On cross-examination, the defense was prohibited from ad- dressing the facts of SR's "bad situation" or "secret," and similarly was prohibited from eliciting factual tes- timony that would inform the members that Appel- lant's efforts to "squash" and "suppress" rumors spe- cifically meant spreading false information provided by SR, on SR's behalf.[11] The result was that the Govern- ment was allowed to portray SR as an innocent victim of an extortionist plot, while the defense was not al- lowed to portray the witness as the architect of a scheme of false allegations intended to cover up her own misconduct. I cannot agree that SR's privacy in- terest in shielding her alleged false statements from inquiry was so important that it justified denying Ap- pellant the opportunity to pierce the veneer of the Gov- ernment's conclusory assertions that were used to con- vict him. I disagree with the notion that M.R.E. 412 was intended to allow the Government to prove the *corpus delicti* of the offenses through a witness indulg- ing in euphemisms of doubtful legal sufficiency, particu-

---

[11] The record of trial is devoid of any facts that would have explained to the members what these words actually meant.

larly when they obscure facts that raise serious ques- tions concerning her own credibility.[12]

When a constitutional violation is shown, a case must be reversed unless the error is harmless beyond a reasonable doubt. *United States v. Israel*, 60 M.J. 485, 488 (C.A.A.F. 2005). In deciding whether or not the er- roneous exclusion of evidence is harmless, the court must consider "the importance of the witness' testi- mony in the prosecution's case, whether the testimony was cumulative, the presence or absence of evidence corroborating or contradicting the testimony of the witness on materials points, the extent of cross- examination otherwise permitted, and ... the strength of the prosecution's case." *United States v. Moss*, 63 M.J. 233, 238 (C.A.A.F. 2006) (*quoting Bahr*, 33 M.J. 228 at 234 (quoting *Delaware v. Van Arsdall*, 465 U.S. 673, 684 (1986))). At trial, SR testified that on 19 October 2005, she had discussed her secret with Appellant in the mailroom; that Appellant had responded by indicat- ing he needed "motivation" to keep "helping her" by continuing to suppress rumors that were circulating about her; that she had replied by asking whether by "motivation" he meant sex—a suggestion she says

---

[12] Certainly there were less burdensome remedies available to the military judge that could have protected the legitimate pri- vacy interests of the victim in this case. The military judge could have fashioned an order restricting the defense from probing the intimate and personal details of the secret, focusing instead on the nature of the encounter and the alleged false claim of sexual as- sault. In addition, the military judge could have closed the pro- ceeding during testimony on the May 2005 incident to protect the victim from undue embarrassment or humiliation. The military judge also could have provided instructions to the members limit- ing the improper use of the evidence.

made him bristle; that Appellant later appeared in her room in Chase Hall on three separate occasions, where they posed together nude for a photograph and en- gaged in sexual activity; that the sexual encounter had in her mind provided the "motivation" Appellant needed to continue to suppress her secret; and that al- though she never told Appellant to stop, she partici- pated only out of fear that he would not keep her se- cret.

Appellant presented his case upon his own testi- mony, stating in substance that while he met SR in the mailroom on 19 October, he never extorted sexual fa- vors from her and denied saying that he needed "moti- vation" to continue suppressing rumors about SR's se- [570]cret. Appellant testified that they discussed get- ting together to pose for a nude photograph in her room; that after arriving in her room that evening, he took two digital photographs of them together, which he kept for safekeeping; and that he subsequently re- turned to her room on two additional occasions to ex- change massages and perform consensual oral sodomy. Appellant admitted that SR was "tense" and "stressed" but claimed that the entire sexual encounter with SR was consensual. (R. at 1325.)

The difficulty accepting Appellant's account of a consensual encounter with SR is that it makes little in- tuitive sense given the lack of any evidence of a rela- tionship or any rational explanation for its spontaneous nature. In short, Appellant's testimony is remarkable in its failure to explain SR's actions in the absence of at least some undue influence. In this failure, however, lies the major flaw in the military judge's M.R.E. 412 order. Appellant's account of an almost spontaneous consensual encounter with SR would be difficult to be- lieve unless the members were informed of SR's prior false claim and were able to understand the depths of her concern for protecting her career. Only if informed of SR's prior scheme would the members have consid- ered the possibility that her encounter with Appellant in October 2005 resulted not so much from coercion, but rather from her own calculation that she needed to en- sure his continued cooperation in keeping her prior misconduct secret. Only then would the members have considered the possibility that SR might have fabri- cated a false claim of sexual assault against Appellant as a preemptive strike, out of fear that the encounter would be discovered through an ongoing investigation. The erroneous M.R.E. 412 order deprived Appellant of his best defense to the charges involving SR.

See United States v. Gray, 40 M.J. 77, 80 (C.M.A. 1994) (military judge committed reversible error by exclud- ing evidence of victim's past sexual behavior under M.R.E. 412; case came down to a credibility contest be- tween witnesses, and the excluded evidence "could have made [the accused's] otherwise incredible expla- nation believable"); *see also United States v. Williams,* 37 M.J. 352, 360 (C.M.A. 1993) (accused's constitutional right to present evidence of victim's extramarital affair improperly excluded under M.R.E. 412; excluded evi- dence would have revealed motive to provide false tes- timony in order to protect affair, victim was key wit- ness in government's case, and evidence of guilt was not overwhelming).

Here, the Government offered no other evidence to support SR's testimony that her sexual encounter with Appellant, which had many outward indicators of being consensual, actually resulted from coercion.

The ad- mission of evidence that SR had furnished Appellant with false information which he then used to counter a career-threatening rumor may well have cast doubt on the veracity of SR's testimony, and tipped the balance in favor of Appellant's version of events. Accordingly, **I** would find that the error in excluding this evidence was not harmless beyond a reasonable doubt.

I would affirm the findings of guilty to sodomy, at- tempted failure to obey a lawful order, and unauthor- ized absence. **I** would set aside the findings of guilty to extortion and indecent assault, and the sentence, and return the case to the Convening Authority for a re- hearing.

For the Court,

Jane R.
Lee
Clerk of the Court

GENERAL COURT-MARTIAL UNITED
STATES COAST GUARD

UNITED STATES

v

.

WEBSTER M. SMITH, CADET, U.S. COAST GUARD

FILED UNDER SEAL[*]

MEMORANDUM ORDER AND OPINION

M.R.E. 413 [sic]

EVIDENCE CADET

[SR]

The Defense has provided notice that it intends to introduce evidence of specific instances of sexual be- havior involving then Cadet, now Ensign [SR].

This alleged sexual behavior is the subject of the secret that Cadet Smith is charged with threatening to expose in Specification **I** of Additional Charge **II**. The Govern- ment seeks to bar the introduction of such evidence pursuant to M.R.E. 412.   At the Article 39(a) session   held on 23 May 2006, Ensign [SR] did not testify be- cause she invoked her right under Article 31(b) to con- sult with an attorney. The accused testified as to the content of his conversations with Cadet [SR] on this subject. The Defense also submitted   a written state- ment dated 15 February 2006 that Cadet [SR] provided to the Coast Guard Investigative Service.

[* Petitioner notes that by order dated October 29, 2009, the court of appeals unsealed this order. Petitioner has nonetheless changed all uses of the accuser's name to her initials.]

FINDINGS OF FACT

During the summer training program at the start of their first class year, Cadet Smith and Cadet [SR] were both assigned to patrol boats that moored at Sta- tion Little Creek. Both lived in barracks rooms at the Station. In May 2005, Cadet Smith approached Cadet [SR] to inform her that he was hearing rumors from the enlisted personnel assigned to the Station that she had a sexual encounter with an enlisted member assigned to the Station. Cadet [SR] told him that this was true, but that it was not a consensual encounter.

Cadet Smith then informed the enlisted personnel who were spreading the rumors that the conduct was not consen- sual.

On or about 19 October 2005, Cadet Smith again approached Cadet [SR]. He told her that he had re- mained in contact with some of the enlisted personnel assigned to Station Little Creek and that the rumors surrounding her sexual encounter with the enlisted man had continued. This time she told him that the in- cident with the enlisted man had been a consensual en- counter and that scope of the encounter had been greater than she had previously described.

At the Article 32 hearing, Cadet [SR] merely stated that she had confided a secret to Cadet Smith. In her 15 February 2006 statement, she merely stated that a situation occurred which led to rumors. On both occasions, she went on to state that on October 19th, she was concerned enough that Cadet Smith would ex- pose this secret that she agreed to pose for a picture with him in which both of them were nude, and later that night allowed him to perform cunnilingus on her then she performed fellatio on him.

CONCLUSIONS OF LAW

1. Generally, evidence that an alleged victim of a sexual offense engaged in other sexual behavior or evi- dence of the alleged victim's sexual predisposition is not admissible. M.R.E. 412(a). There are three excep- tions to this general rule, but only one may be relevant here: evidence of the sexual behavior of the victim is admissible if excluding the evidence would violate the constitutional rights of the accused. M.R.E. 412(b)(1)(C). This exception protects the accused's Sixth Amendment right to confront witnesses and Fifth Amendment right to a fair trial. *United States v. Banker*, 60 M.J. 216, 221 (2004). In other words, the ac-cused has a right to produce relevant evidence that is material and favorable to his defense. *Id.* Evidence is relevant if it tends to make the existence of any fact more or less probable than it would be without the evi- dence. M.R.E. 401. Assuming these requirements are met, the accused must also demonstrate that the proba- tive value of the evidence outweighs the danger of un- fair prejudice. M.R.E. 412(c)(3). In this context, the unfair prejudice is, in part, to the privacy interests of the alleged victim. *Banker*, 60 M.J. at 223. M.R.E. 412 is a legislative recognition of the high value we as a so-

ciety place on keeping our sexual behavior private.

2. The Defense offered several theories of why this evidence is admissible. First, the Defense wanted to introduce this evidence to impeach the credibility of Ensign [SR] when she testifies. The general rule is that a witness' credibility may be attacked in the form of an opinion or by reputation concerning the witness' character for truthfulness. M.R.E. 608(a). Specific in- stances of conduct of witness may be admitted, at the discretion of the military judge, if probative of truth- fulness. **I** decline to exercise that discretion in this case

because **I** believe that, under these circumstances, the probative value of this evidence is substantially out- weighed by the danger of unfair prejudice. Then Cadet [SR] was under no duty to be completely forthcoming with Cadet Smith concerning her private life, particu- larly under these circumstances since her rumored con- duct would be in violation of Coast Guard regulations and could subject her to disciplinary action or other ad- verse consequences. More important, despite any limit- ing instruction, members might consider this evidence less for its tendency to prove Ensign [SR]'s character for truthfulness than for its tendency to prove that she is a bad person. Finally, conflicting testimony on this point from Ensign [SR] and Cadet Smith could easily sidetrack members from testimony regarding the charged offenses which the member's should be focus- ing on.

3. The Defense also argued that the members must know the substance of Cadet [SR]'s secret in or- der for them to independently assess whether or not she would feel coerced into taking a nude photograph with Cadet Smith and later engaging in mutual oral sex in order to protect that secret. While the importance of her secret would be relevant in this fashion, **I** do not think that the members would need to know the specif- ics. At the Article 39(a) session, the Government of- fered a generic formulation that would impress upon the members the seriousness of the secret. In essence, the members could be informed that the secret was in- formation that if revealed could have an adverse impact on her Coast Guard career, including possibly discipli- nary action under the UCMJ.

4. The final rationale offered by the Defense at the Article 39(a) hearing is the most persuasive. The Defense argued that if the members hear that Cadet

[SR] originally told Cadet Smith that a sexual encoun- ter with another man was non-consensual, and then later admitted that it in fact was consensual, then the members could use this testimony to infer that the same thing is happening in this case. In other words, the members could infer that Cadet [SR] has a propensity to bring false accusations against men with whom she has had consensual sexual encounters. I agree that this theory would be a valid reason for admitting this evidence under M.R.E. 412(b)(1)(C), but there are two problems with the Defense proffer. First, the evidence proffered that Cadet [SR] made these statements is not strong since it comes from the accused, who has an ob- vious bias. Cadet [SR]'s written statement and Article 32 testimony on this point is not clear. She admitted at the Article 32 that she only partially confided in Cadet

Smith in May and fully confided in him on October 19th; however, this is far from proof that she initially claimed that the encounter was non-consensual.

In fact, it is consistent with the rest of Cadet Smith's Article 39(a) testimony that on October 19th she told him that the scope of the sexual encounter had been greater than she had previously described. The probative value of this evidence is therefore low.

5. More important, there is no evidence that Ca- det [SR] made an official complaint against the un- named enlisted man. Even if Cadet [SR] told the ac- cused in May that the encounter was not consensual, the nature of this confidential statement is far different from the nature of her statements to law enforcement personnel that she must have known would result in a public prosecution. Cadet [SR]'s alleged statement to Cadet Smith was apparently intended to keep more people from learning about her sexual encounter with the enlisted man. It was not a false complaint to law

enforcement. In contrast, her statements made in this case were to law enforcement personal and would cer- tainly lead to a public prosecution. Consequently, even if Cadet [SR] falsely told the accused *in confidence* that her sexual encounter with the enlisted man was non- consensual *in an effort to suppress rumors*, this would have little value in proving that her *official* allegations against Cadet Smith *resulting in a public trial* are also false. **I** am convinced that the minimal probative value of this evidence is outweighed by danger of unfair prejudice to Ensign [SR]'s privacy interests and the potential danger of sidetracking the member's atten- tion to a collateral issue as described in paragraph 2 above.

5. For the above reasons, the Government's ob- jection that this evidence is inadmissible in accordance with **M.R.E. 413** [sic] is **SUSTAINED**.

EFFECTIVE DATE

This order was effective on 26 May 2006.

Done at Washington, DC,

/
s
/

Brian Judge
Captain, U.S. Coast Guard
Military Judge

APPENDIX D

IN THE UNITED STATES COAST
GUARD COURT OF CRIMINAL
APPEALS

Docket No. 1275
CGCMG 0224

UNITED STATES,
Appellee

v.

WEBSTER M. SMITH, CADET, U.S. COAST GUARD,
Appellant

---

14 May 2008

APPELLANT'S MOTION FOR
RECONSIDERATION EN BANC
FILED 9 MAY 2008

ORDER

Appellant filed a Motion for Reconsideration En Banc, and for leave to file a brief in support thereof. On consideration of Appellant's Motion, filed under the Court's Rules of Practice and Procedure, it is, by the Court, this 14th day of May, 2008,

ORDERED:

That Appellant's Motion be, and the same is, hereby denied.

For the Court,

L. I. McClelland
Chief Judge

Copy: Office of Military Justice
           Appellate Government
           Counsel Appellate
           Defense Counsel

Appendix 10

Decision of Court of Appeals for the Armed Forces (CAAF)

UNITED STATES, Appellee
v.
Webster M. SMITH, Cadet
U.S. Coast Guard, Appellant

No. 08-0719
Crim. App. No. 1275
United States Court of Appeals for the Armed Forces

November 10, 2009
March 29, 2010

STUCKY, J., delivered the judgment of the Court, in which RYAN, J., joined. BAKER, J., filed a separate opinion concurring in the result. ERDMANN, J., filed a separate opinion concurring in part and dissenting in part, in which EFFRON, C.J., joined.

Counsel For Appellant: Ronald C. Machen, Esq. (argued); Commander Necia L. Chambliss, Will L. Crossley, Esq., and Daniel S. Volchok, Esq. (on brief); Lieutenant Robert M. Pirone and Stuart F. Delery, Esq.

For Appellee: Lieutenant Emily P. Reuter (argued); Commander Stephen P. McCleary, Lieutenant Commander Brian K. Koshulsky, and Lieutenant Alfred J. Thompson.
Military Judge: Brian M. Judge

THIS OPINION IS SUBJECT TO REVISION BEFORE FINAL PUBLICATION.

United States v. Smith, No. 08-0719/CG

Judge STUCKY delivered the judgment of the Court.

At trial, the military judge limited Appellant's crossexamination of Cadet SR, the Government's only witness on his three convictions related to sexual misconduct. We granted review to decide whether Appellant was denied his right to confront his accuser on those three specifications. We hold that Appellant was not denied his right to confront his accuser, and affirm.

I.

A general court-martial consisting of members convicted Appellant, contrary to his pleas, of attempting to disobey an order, going from his place of duty, sodomy, extortion, and indecent assault. Articles 80, 86, 125, 127, and 134, Uniform Code of Military Justice (UCMJ), 10 U.S.C. §§ 880, 886, 925, 927, 934 (2006). The convening authority approved the sentence the members adjudged: a dismissal, confinement for six months, and forfeiture of all pay and allowances. The United States Coast Guard Court of Criminal Appeals affirmed on April 9, 2008. United States v. Smith, 66 M.J. 556, 563 (C.G. Ct. Crim. App. 2008). Appellant filed a motion for reconsideration which was denied on May 14, 2008. Appellant petitioned this Court for review on July 14, 2008.

2

II.

As a preliminary matter, the Government contends that Appellant's petition for review was not timely filed, and that therefore the grant of review should be dismissed as improvidently granted. Article 67(b), UCMJ, 10 U.S.C. § 867(b) (2006), provides that an accused has sixty days to petition this Court for review from the earlier of "(1) the date on which the accused is notified of the decision of the Court of Criminal Appeals; or (2) the date on which a copy of the decision . . . , after being served on appellate counsel of record for the accused . . . is deposited in the United States mails for delivery by first class certified mail to the accused." In United States v. Rodriguez, we held that the sixty-day statutory
period for filing petitions for review was jurisdictional and could not be waived. 67 M.J. 110, 116 (C.A.A.F. 2009).

Before filing a petition for review at this Court,
Appellant timely sought reconsideration of the CCA's decision. Until the CCA rendered a decision on the reconsideration request, either by denying reconsideration or by granting reconsideration and rendering a new decision, there was no CCA decision for this Court to review. We hold that Appellant's sixty-day period for filing at this Court began on the date the defense was formally notified, under the provisions of Article 67(b), UCMJ, of the CCA's decision on reconsideration. The

3

evidence of record does not support the Government's contention that the appeal was untimely filed.

III.

Appellant and Cadet SR were cadets at the United States Coast Guard Academy. During the summer of 2005, Cadet SR and Appellant were assigned to neighboring Coast Guard cutters in Norfolk, Virginia. While there, Cadet SR committed an indiscretion that could have jeopardized her ranking as a cadet and threatened her Coast Guard career. Shortly thereafter, Appellant sent her a text message saying that he hoped the rumors he was hearing were not true. Cadet SR discussed the situation with Appellant but lied about some of the details. Appellant "said he'd try to squash rumors, and that it would be okay." In October of that year, after both had returned to the Academy, Appellant notified Cadet SR that the rumors were persisting. She then truthfully disclosed the details of her indiscretion. Appellant said he would continue to try to suppress the rumors, but that he needed motivation to do so. Appellant denied he was seeking sexual favors but suggested the couple take a photograph of themselves naked together to build "trust in one another." After the photo, Appellant left but returned to her room later that evening. On this occasion, he

4

inserted his fingers in her vagina and placed his tongue on her clitoris. Cadet SR then performed fellatio on him.

IV.

Appellant alleged that Cadet SR's indiscretion involved engaging in sex with an enlisted member and, pursuant to Military Rule of Evidence (M.R.E.) 412(c)(1), Appellant moved to admit evidence of this prior sexual conduct. That rule provides that "[e]vidence offered to prove that any alleged victim engaged in other sexual behavior" is not generally admissible. M.R.E. 412(a)(1). However, "evidence the exclusion of which would violate the constitutional rights of the accused" is admissible. M.R.E. 412(b)(1)(C). During a closed hearing conducted pursuant to M.R.E. 412(c)(2), Appellant testified that in May 2005 Cadet SR told him that she had had nonconsensual sexual encounters with an enlisted member, but that in October 2005 she admitted that those sexual encounters had actually been consensual. Cadet SR invoked her right against self-incrimination and did not testify at the hearing. Appellant argued that he should be allowed to question Cadet SR about the encounters for "the specific purpose of establishing a pattern of lying about sexual events." The military judge sustained the Government's objection to the admission of this evidence, but allowed the "members [to] be informed that [Cadet SR's] secret was information that if

5

revealed could have an adverse impact on her Coast Guard career, including possibly disciplinary action under the UCMJ." The CCA affirmed this decision. Smith, 66 M.J. at 560-61. Appellant asserts that the military judge erred in not admitting the sexual nature of Cadet SR's indiscretion, and requests that we set aside his convictions for extortion, sodomy, and indecent acts.

V.

The Sixth Amendment provides that "[i]n all criminal prosecutions, the accused shall enjoy the right . . . to be confronted with the witnesses against him." U.S. Const. amend. VI. The right to confrontation includes the right of a military accused to cross-examine adverse witnesses. See United States v. Clayton, 67 M.J. 283, 287 (C.A.A.F. 2009). Uncovering and presenting to court members "a witness' motivation in testifying is a proper and important function of the constitutionally protected right of cross-examination." Davis v. Alaska, 415 U.S. 308, 316 (1974) (citation omitted). "Through crossexamination, an accused can 'expose to the jury the facts from which jurors . . . could appropriately draw inferences relating to the reliability of the witness.'" United States v. Collier, 67 M.J. 347, 352 (C.A.A.F. 2009) (quoting Davis, 415 U.S. at 318).

6

Typically, we review a military judge's decision to admit
or exclude evidence for an abuse of discretion. See United
States v. Weston, 67 M.J. 390, 392 (C.A.A.F. 2009). We have also applied the abuse of discretion standard to alleged
violations of the Sixth Amendment Confrontation Clause. United States v. Moss, 63
M.J. 233, 236 (C.A.A.F. 2006); United States v. Israel, 60 M.J. 485, 488 (C.A.A.F. 2005).
Appellant has the burden under M.R.E. 412 of establishing
his entitlement to any exception to the prohibition on the
admission of evidence "offered to prove that any alleged victim engaged in other sexual conduct." United States v. Banker, 60 M.J. 216, 218, 223 (C.A.A.F. 2004) (citation omitted). To establish that the excluded evidence "would violate the constitutional rights of the accused," M.R.E. 412(b)(1)(C), an accused must demonstrate that the evidence is relevant, material, and favorable to his defense, "and thus whether it is 'necessary.'" Id. at 222 (quoting United States v. Williams, 37 M.J. 352, 361 (C.M.A. 1993)). The term "'favorable'" as used in both Supreme Court and military precedent is synonymous with "'vital.'" Id. (quoting United States v. Valenzuela-Bernal, 458 U.S. 858, 867 (1982); United States v. Dorsey, 16 M.J. 1, 8 (C.M.A. 1983)).

Appellant contends that his inability to cross-examine
Cadet SR about the nature of the secret affected his convictions

7

for sodomy, extortion, and committing an indecent act. We
conclude that further cross-examination of Cadet SR was not "constitutionally
required." Assuming arguendo that the exact nature of the indiscretion -- that it
involved consensual sexual relations with an enlisted member -- was relevant, it was
neither material nor vital to Appellant's defense.
Testimony is material if it was "'of consequence to the
determination of' appellant's guilt." Dorsey, 16 M.J. at 6
(quoting M.R.E. 401). In determining whether evidence is of
consequence to the determination of Appellant's guilt, we
"consider the importance of the issue for which the evidence was offered in relation to
the other issues in this case; the extent to which this issue is in dispute; and the
nature of other evidence in the case pertaining to this issue." Id. (citation omitted). In
this case, the evidence was offered on a
significant issue, the alleged victim's credibility, which was
in dispute. Nevertheless, knowledge of the exact nature of her indiscretion in relation
to the other issues in the case was not important. The military judge allowed Appellant
to present a fairly precise and plausible theory of bias, i.e., that she lied to preserve a
secret which "if revealed could have an adverse impact on her Coast Guard career,
including possibly disciplinary action under the UCMJ." While Cadet SR'scredibility
was in contention, it is unclear why the lurid

8

nuances of her sexual past would have added much to Appellant's extant theory of fabrication.

Nor is cross-examining Cadet SR about her sexual past "'vital'" under Banker, 60 M.J. at 222 (quoting Valenzuela-Bernal, 458 U.S. at 867; Dorsey, 16 M.J. at 8)). The "vital" issue is not whether Cadet SR engaged in consensual sex with an enlisted member or whether she lied to Appellant about it, but rather whether she lied about an important issue that would impeach her credibility. Cadet SR admitted that she had been in a "situation" that could have jeopardized her career and her ranking as a cadet; that the "situation" was in violation of cadet regulations and possibly a violation of the UCMJ; and that she initially lied to Appellant about the "situation." All of this was before the members. The military judge did not abuse his discretion; he provided Appellant what he was due under the Confrontation Clause: an opportunity to impeach the complainant's credibility.

Finally, Appellant argues that Cadet SR's past indiscretion and her lies about it gave her similar motive to lie about her relationship with Appellant. We decline to embrace such a broad, cumulative reading of M.R.E. 412 and its case law. Even according to Appellant's own theory, Cadet SR lied about her sexual past to protect herself, not a relationship with another, unlike United States v. Williams, 37 M.J. 352 (C.M.A. 1993), or

United States v. Smith, No. 08-0719/CG

Olden v. Kentucky, 488 U.S. 227 (1988). This is not a case like Collier in which the appellant asserted she was framed for larceny by her gay lover after the breakup of the relationship. 67 M.J. at 351. Nor does this case involve recent extramarital sex or rejection and invective which might have caused the victim to falsely claim rape, as in Dorsey, 16 M.J. at 6. To the extent Appellant might have tried to introduce some nonsexual aspects of his theory of bias via M.R.E. 608(c), he failed to frame or raise this issue as such at trial.

VI.

The decision of the United States Coast Guard Court of Criminal Appeals is affirmed.

10

United States v. Smith, No. 08-0719/CG

BAKER, Judge (concurring in the result):
I concur in the result. In my view, this case is governed
by United States v. Banker, 60 M.J. 216, 225 (C.A.A.F. 2004).
In Banker, we concluded that in the context of Military Rule of Evidence (M.R.E.) 412, it is "within the judge's discretion to determine that such a cursory argument [does] not sufficiently articulate how the testimony reasonably established a motive to fabricate. . . . [It is] within the discretion of the military judge to conclude that the offered testimony was not relevant." Id. at 225. The burden is on the appellant to prove why the M.R.E. 412 prohibition should be lifted. Id.
Appellant's theory of admission was that SR, having lied to
Appellant about her prior sexual misconduct with an enlisted member of the Coast Guard, demonstrated a propensity to lie about her sex life generally and in particular to make false allegations to law enforcement authorities to conceal her own sexual misconduct. Appellant argues that SR's misconduct also included engaging in consensual sexual activities with Appellant
in the Cadet barracks. Therefore, Appellant argues, he had a constitutional right to cross-examine SR about her prior sexual conduct, notwithstanding the general prohibition on such examination enshrined in M.R.E. 412.
The problem for Appellant is that his theory of admission
is too far-fetched to pass constitutional and M.R.E. 403 muster.

First, SR had no obligation to tell Appellant about her sexual life and misconduct. It does not logically follow that someone who would lie to protect her privacy from a probing acquaintance would lie to the police and commit perjury. Second, it was SR herself who reported her sexual contact with Appellant; this cuts against Appellant's theory that SR would lie to conceal her own misconduct. Third, to support this theory of admission the members needed to know that SR had "lied" to Appellant about her sexual misconduct; they did not need to know the details of the prior sexual conduct. This much the military judge permitted.

In my view, Appellant might have a different appellate case if he had argued to this Court that members needed to know the nature of "the secret" in order to assess beyond a reasonable doubt whether SR might succumb to pressure to protect the secret. This alternative theory was not the basis of Appellant's appeal before this Court. In any event, it should be noted that the military judge rejected this theory at trial, his conclusions of law stating:

While the importance of her secret would be relevant in this fashion, I do not think that the members would need to know the specifics. At the Article 39(a) session, the Government offered a generic formulation that would impress upon the members the seriousness of the secret. In essence, the members could be informed that the secret was information that if revealed could have an adverse impact on her Coast Guard career, including possibly disciplinary action under the UCMJ.

2

United States v. Smith, No. 08-0719/CG

Reasonable judges might disagree on whether additional detail about "the secret" was needed for members to fairly assess whether this Coast Guard cadet was coerced into sexual conduct to safeguard that secret. But I am not persuaded that it was plain error. The military judge informed the members that the secret exposed the witness to criminal liability and violated academy regulations. This is the very sort of balancing military judges are supposed to conduct when they weigh an accused's rights and a victim's privacy under M.R.E. 412.

3

United States v. Smith, No. 08-0719/CG

ERDMANN, Judge, with whom EFFRON, Chief Judge, joins(concurring in part and dissenting in part):

While I concur with the majority opinion as to the jurisdictional issue raised by the Government, I respectfully dissent from the majority's conclusion as to the granted issue.

In a case where credibility of the complainant was fundamental, the military judge prevented the defense from presenting to the panel an explanation of the circumstances that would have provided a motive for the complainant to make a false allegation of rape.

Background

Cadet Webster Smith was initially charged with twenty-two specifications, the majority of which related to his sexual relationships with female cadets at the United States Coast Guard Academy. Eleven of those charges were dismissed before trial. At a general court-martial composed of members, Smith was found not guilty of six of the remaining charges. Contrary to his pleas, the members found him guilty of absence without leave, attempted failure to obey a lawful order, sodomy, extortion, and indecent assault. The sodomy, extortion, and indecent assault charges arose out of allegations made by SR, a female cadet.

In this appeal, Smith asserts that the military judge erred by preventing him from fully cross-examining SR as to her motive and credibility in violation of his Sixth Amendment right to confrontation and the "constitutionally required" exception to Military Rule of Evidence (M.R.E.) 412. M.R.E. 412(b)(1)(C). At trial the defense filed a motion pursuant to M.R.E. 412 requesting permission to cross-examine SR about her alleged statements to Smith concerning a prior sexual encounter she had with an enlisted servicemember. The factual basis for the motion was summarized by the military judge in his findings of fact:

> During the summer training program at the start of their first class year, Cadet Smith and [SR] were both assigned to patrol boats that moored at Station Little Creek. Both lived in barracks rooms at the Station. In May 2005, Cadet Smith approached [SR] to inform her that he was hearing rumors from the enlisted personnel assigned to the Station that she had a sexual encounter with an enlisted member assigned to the Station. [SR] told him that this was true, but that it was not a consensual encounter. Cadet Smith then informed the enlisted personnel who were spreading the rumors that the conduct was not consensual. On or about 19 October 2005, Cadet Smith again approached [SR]. He told her that he had remained in contact with some of the enlisted personnel assigned to Station Little Creek and that the rumors surrounding her sexual encounter with the enlisted man had continued. This time she told him that the incident with the enlisted man had been a consensual encounter and that the scope of the encounter had been greater than she had previously described. At the Article 32 hearing, [SR] merely stated that she had confided a secret to Cadet Smith. In her 15 February 2006 statement, she merely stated that a situation occurred which led to rumors. On both occasions, she went on to state that on October 19th,

2

> she was concerned enough that Cadet Smith would expose
> this secret that she agreed to pose for a picture with
> him in which both of them were nude, and later that
> night allowed him to perform cunnilingus on her then
> she performed fellatio on him.

In the defense motion, Smith argued that the evidence was constitutionally required because "[t]he fact that the alleged victim lied to Cadet Smith about her sexual activity and has misled CGIS about that activity tends to show the alleged victim as untruthful about her sexual conduct generally and specifically has motive to lie about the specific sexual rumors underlying the charge -- the very issue before the trier of fact."

The Government opposed the admission of the evidence arguing that the substance of SR's secret was not relevant, material, or vital to Smith's defense. In denying the motion

the military judge concluded that: while the evidence was relevant, the members did not need to know the specifics, but could be provided with a non-specific summary[2]; although the evidence could show that SR had a propensity to bring false accusations against men with whom she had consensual sexual encounters, the evidence was not strong since the source of the allegation, Smith, was biased; there was a significant

---

[2] The military judge found that "the members could be informed that the secret was information that if revealed could have an adverse impact on [SR's] Coast Guard career, including possibly disciplinary action under the UCMJ."

United States v. Smith, No. 08-0719/CG

difference between SR making a false allegation to Smith and making a false allegation to law enforcement authorities; and the probative value of the evidence was outweighed by the danger of unfair prejudice.
The United States Coast Guard Court of Criminal Appeals
affirmed the findings and sentence. United States v. Smith, 66 M.J. 556, 563 (C.G. Ct. Crim. App. 2008). We review a military judge's decision to admit or exclude evidence for an abuse of discretion. United States v. Ayala, 43 M.J. 296, 298 (C.A.A.F. 1995). In doing so, we review findings of fact under the clearly erroneous standard and conclusions of law under the de novo standard. Id.

Discussion

The evidence at issue was proffered to attack SR's
credibility by establishing that she had earlier made a false
allegation of a nonconsensual sexual encounter to protect her Coast Guard career. Before addressing the M.R.E. 412 issue, it is worth noting that there is some question as to whether M.R.E. 412 even applies to this type of evidence. The Drafters' Analysis to M.R.E. 412 states "[e]vidence of past false complaints of sexual offenses by an alleged victim of a sexual offense is not within the scope of this Rule and is not objectionable when otherwise admissible." Manual for Courts- Martial, United States, Analysis of the Military Rules of

4

United States v. Smith, No. 08-0719/CG

Evidence app. 22 at A22-36 (2008 ed.).[3] However, given the
posture of this case on appeal, and assuming that M.R.E. 412 does apply, the evidence
is clearly admissible under the M.R.E. 412 analysis.

1. Objections Under M.R.E. 412
"[A] criminal defendant states a violation of the
Confrontation Clause by showing that he was prohibited from engaging in otherwise
appropriate cross-examination designed to show a prototypical form of bias on the part
of the witness, and thereby 'to expose to the jury the facts from which jurors . . . could
appropriately draw inferences relating to the reliability of the witness.'" Delaware v.
Van Arsdall, 475 U.S. 673, 680 (1986) (citing Davis v. Alaska, 415 U.S. 308, 318
(1974)).
"[E]xposure of a witness' motivation in testifying is a proper
and important function of the constitutionally protected right of cross-examination."
Id. at 678-79. "The question is whether '[a] reasonable jury might have received a
significantly different impression of [the witness's] credibility had [defense counsel]
been permitted to pursue his proposed line of crossexamination.'" United States v.
Collier, 67 M.J. 347, 352

---

[3] See also Fed. R. Evid. 412 advisory committee's note on proposed 1994 amendment
("Evidence offered to prove allegedly false prior claims by the victim is not barred by
Rule 412. However, the evidence is subject to the requirements of Rule 404.").

(C.A.A.F. 2009) (brackets in original) (quoting Van Arsdall, 475 U.S. at 680).
"M.R.E. 412 was intended to protect victims of sexual
offenses from the degrading and embarrassing disclosure of
intimate details of their private lives while preserving the
constitutional rights of the accused to present a defense."
United States v. Banker, 60 M.J. 216, 219 (C.A.A.F 2004). There are, however, three
exceptions to the exclusionary provisions of M.R.E. 412. Smith relied on the third
exception that requires the admission of evidence "the exclusion of which would
violatethe constitutional rights of the accused." M.R.E. 412(b)(1)(C).
"This exception addresses an accused's Sixth Amendment right of confrontation and
Fifth Amendment right to a fair trial." Banker, 60 M.J. at 221 (citations omitted)
(emphasis added).
Banker requires that "where evidence is offered pursuant to this exception, it is
important for defense counsel to detail an accused's theory of relevance and
constitutional necessity." 60 M.J. at 221. Smith's counsel did just that in this case.

2. Relevance and Materiality
In order to properly determine whether evidence is
admissible under the constitutionally required exception the
military judge must evaluate whether the proffered evidence is relevant, material, and
favorable to the defense. Id. at 222.
"[T]he relevancy portion of this test is the same as that

6

employed for the other two exceptions of the rule," which is
that "[e]vidence is relevant if it has 'any tendency to make the existence of any fact . . .
more probable or less probable than it would be without the evidence.' M.R.E. 401." Id.
at 222.

The proffered evidence could have impacted SR's credibility by allowing the defense to
provide a commonsense explanation for SR to give false testimony. That is, when SR
learned of the investigation of Smith for alleged sexual offenses, she became concerned
that the investigation would produce allegations that she had engaged in prohibited
sexual activity[4] with Smith in their dormitory at the Coast Guard Academy, thereby
jeopardizing her own career. Thus, she fabricated the charges against Smith to protect
her career, as she had in the past for the same reason. The military judge found that
the evidence would be relevant and I agree.

Having found the evidence relevant, the next step for the military judge was to
determine whether the evidence was "material and favorable to the accused's defense,
and thus
whether it is 'necessary'." Id. at 222 (citing United States v. Williams, 37 M.J. 352, 361
(C.M.A. 1993)).

7

---

[4] 3 Pursuant to Regulations for the Code of Cadets 4-5-05.a.3, sexual conduct is
prohibited on Coast Guard Academy installations even if it is between consenting
cadets. Cadets found guilty of consensual sexual misconduct can be disenrolled. Id. at
4-5-05.a.4.

> In determining whether evidence is material, the military judge looks at "the importance of the issue for which the evidence was offered in relation to the other issues in this case; the extent to which this issue is in dispute; and the nature of the other evidence in the case pertaining to this issue."

Id. (quoting United States v. Colon-Angueira, 16 M.J. 20, 26 (C.M.A. 1983)).

There can be no dispute that testing the credibility of a witness through cross-examination is crucial to the right of confrontation.

> A more particular attack on the witness' credibility is effected by means of cross-examination directed toward revealing possible biases, prejudices, or ulterior motives of the witness as they may relate directly to issues or personalities in the case at hand. The partiality of a witness is subject to exploration at trial, and is "always relevant as discrediting the witness and affecting the weight of his testimony." 3A J. Wigmore, Evidence § 940, p. 775 (Chadbourn rev. 1970). We have recognized that the exposure of a witness' motivation in testifying is a proper and important function of the constitutionally protected right of cross-examination.

Davis v. Alaska, 415 U.S. 308, 316 (1974) (citation omitted).

As in United States v. Dorsey, 16 M.J. 1, 7 (C.M.A. 1983), this was a "he said -- she said" case and for the charges at issue in this appeal,[5] the critical question for the members was the credibility of the sole prosecution witness. Evidence of a motive to fabricate and that SR had alleged that an earlier consensual sexual encounter was nonconsensual in an attempt to.

8

---

[5] Sodomy, extortion, and indecent assault.

protect her career bears directly on SR's credibility as to the allegations she made against Smith. It may have shown that SR had a propensity to lie about consensual sexual encounters when her career was on the line. The materiality of this evidence is not the "lurid nuances of the victim's sexual past" as noted by the majority, but rather the allegation that SR had previously lied about a sexual encounter under similar circumstances.

3. Balancing

Once the military judge has determined that the proffered evidence is relevant and material, the military judge must undertake the M.R.E. 412 balancing test to determine if the evidence is favorable to the accused's defense[6]. Banker, 60 M.J. at 222. The term favorable is synonymous with vital. Id. "[W]hen balancing the probative value of the evidence against the danger of unfair prejudice under M.R.E. 412, the military judge must consider . . . factors such as confusion of the issues, misleading the members, undue delay, waste of time,

9

---

[6] Commentators have noted that the "constitutionally required" exception may be unnecessary since once it is established that the evidence is constitutionally required, there can be no further limitation on its admission. See 1 Stephen A. Saltzburg et al., Military Rules of Evidence Manual § 412.02[4], at 4-194 (6th ed. 2006) ("Any limitation on a constitutional right would be disregarded whether or not such a Rule existed."); Christopher B. Mueller & Laird C. Kirkpatrick, Federal Evidence § 4:81, at 306 (3d ed. 2007) ("The exception is arguably unnecessary because Fed. R. Evid. 412 is subordinate to the Constitution anyway, but perhaps including it diminishes the sense of conflict between the two legal standards.").

needless presentation of cumulative evidence, [and] also
prejudice to the victim's legitimate privacy interests." Id. at
223. The M.R.E. 412 balancing test weighs in Smith's favor.
Under the circumstances of this case, any risk of confusion of the issues, misleading
the members, wasting time, or presenting cumulative evidence was minimal and is
outweighed by the high probative value of this evidence.
In Dorsey the court found evidence favorable when it
"undermined the credibility of the sole prosecution witness who directly testified to
appellant's guilt of the charged offense." Dorsey, 16 M.J. at 7. In a similar fashion,
admission of a prior false allegation of a nonconsensual sexual encounter could have
undermined the credibility of SR, the only witness who testified against Smith on the
extortion, sodomy, and indecent assault charges.
While the evidence of SR's earlier allegation of a false
nonconsensual sexual encounter and her subsequent admission that the encounter
was consensual would have impacted her privacy interests, withholding this
constitutionally required evidence from the panel deprived Smith of his best
opportunity to provide a motive for SR's allegations and to challenge her credibility.
The fact that the military judge allowed the panel to hear that SR had a secret that, if
revealed could have an adverse impact on her Coast Guard career, including possibly
disciplinary

10

action under the UCMJ, was simply not sufficient. With this
limited information about SR's secret, the members were left to speculate whether the
secret was a minor disciplinary infraction or a more serious charge, but they had no
idea that the proffered evidence directly implicated SR's motive and credibility.[7]
In Collier this court found the military judge erred in
limiting cross-examination of the complaining witness for
possible bias. Collier, 67 M.J. at 349. There, the defendant
attempted to establish bias by presenting evidence of the
existence of a romantic relationship that ended badly between the accused and the
complaining witness. Id. at 351. The military judge only allowed cross-examination as
to the "breakup of a friendship." Id. at 351-52. This court found that there was a
qualitative difference between the two situations and if the members had been shown
evidence of the romantic relationship they might have had a significantly different
impression of the accusing witness' credibility. Id. at 352, 353. Similarly, there is a
qualitative difference between an undisclosed

11

---

[7] 6 Trial counsel illustrated the range of incidents that the
members could have speculated on when, at one point during his argument on the
motion, he stated that while the existence of the secret was extremely relevant, the
content of the secret was not. Trial counsel argued, "[t]he extortion charge is that there
was a secret. It doesn't matter if that secret was whether she liked Smarties. It doesn't
matter if she had committed some other felony . . . ."

situation that "could have had an adverse impact on [SR's] Coast Guard career" and an allegation that SR had previously made a false allegation of a nonconsensual sexual encounter to protect her career.

While the military judge found that the evidence was not strong because it came from Smith, who had an obvious bias, it is well established that "[t]he weight and credibility of the . . . witness are matters for the members alone to decide." United States v. Moss, 63 M.J. 233, 239 (C.A.A.F. 2006) (citing United States v.Bins, 43 M.J. 79, 85 (C.A.A.F. 1995)). The court in Banker noted that the role of the military judge is to assure that the evidence meets the usual evidentiary standards. Banker, 60 M.J. at 224 (citing United States v. Platero, 72 F.3d 806, 812 (10th Cir. 1995)). The court in Platero went on to say, "when the Judge decides whether or not a defense is true or false and decides that on the basis of the credibility of the witnesses, the Judge is doing what the jury is supposed to do in a serious criminal case covered by the Sixth Amendment." Platero, 72 F.3d at 812.

Smith had a commonsense explanation for SR's claim that the sexual activity was nonconsensual and the military judge's ruling prevented the members from considering this theory. The alleged false accusation was close in time to the allegation made against Smith, both allegations involved military members

12

and both situations presented a motive for SR to lie about the consensual nature of her sexual activities to protect her
career. Putting aside the fact that M.R.E. 412 may not even apply to this type of evidence, I would conclude that the evidence should have been admitted under M.R.E. 412. I would further find that the error was not harmless beyond a reasonable doubt as it essentially deprived Smith of his best defense and "the excluded evidence may have tipped the credibility balance in [Smith's] favor." Moss, 63 M.J. at 239.
I would reverse the decision of the United States Coast Guard Court of Criminal Appeals and set aside the findings and sentence for Additional Charge I, Specification 1 of Additional Charge II, and Additional Charge III, and remand the case for further proceedings, if any.

Appendix 11

Appeal to the U. S. Supreme Court For A Writ Of Certiarori (with Appendixes)

No. 10-   10-18

IN THE

Supreme Court of the United States

WEBSTER M. SMITH,
Petitioner,

v.

UNITED STATES OF AMERICA,
Respondent.

ON PETITION FOR A WRIT OF CERTIORARI TO THE
UNITED STATES COURT OF APPEALS
FOR THE ARMED FORCES

PETITION FOR A WRIT OF CERTIORARI

DANIEL S. VOLCHOK
Counsel of Record
SETH P. WAXMAN
A. STEPHEN HUT, JR.
EDWARD C. DUMONT
WILMER CUTLER PICKERING
  HALE AND DORR LLP
1875 Pennsylvania Avenue N.W.
Washington, D.C. 20006
(202) 663-6000
daniel.volchok@wilmerhale.com

Blank Page

QUESTION PRESENTED

When a trial judge's restriction on the cross-examination of a prosecution witness is challenged on appeal as a violation of the Confrontation Clause, is the standard of review de novo, as five circuits have held, or abuse of discretion, as six other circuits (and the court of appeals here) have concluded?

(i)

210

Blank Page

TABLE OF CONTENTS

Page

QUESTION PRESENTED...i

TABLE OF AUTHORITIES v

OPINIONS BELOW 1

JURISDICTION..2

CONSTITUTIONAL PROVISION INVOLVED 2

STATEMENT 2

REASONS FOR GRANTING THE PETITION........11

I. CAAF'S STANDARD-OF-REVIEW HOLDING IMPLICATES AN ESTABLISHED CIRCUIT CONFLICT ON AN IMPORTANT AND RECURRING QUESTION OF FEDERAL LAW 12

    A. The Courts Of Appeals Are Deeply Divided Over What Standard Of Review Applies To Confrontation Clause Claims Like Mr. Smith's..12

    B. The Question Presented Is Recurring And Important, And This Case Is A Good Vehicle For Deciding It 14

II. CAAF'S STANDARD-OF-REVIEW HOLDING IS WRONG 16

    A. Under This Court's Precedent, Mixed Questions Of Law And Fact Are Reviewed De Novo When Constitutional Rights Are Involved 17

    B. The Cases Relied On By Courts That Employ Abuse-Of-Discretion Review Do Not Support That Approach 22

CONCLUSION 26

(iii)

TABLE OF CONTENTS—Continued

Page

APPENDIX A: Opinion of the United States Court of Appeals for the Armed Forces 1a

APPENDIX B: Opinion of the United States Coast Guard Court of Criminal Appeals 23a

APPENDIX C: Order of the Military Judge Denying Petitioner's Motion To Conduct the Cross-Examination at Issue 59a

APPENDIX D: Order of the Court of Criminal Appeals Denying Reconsideration En Banc 65a

TABLE OF AUTHORITIES

CASES

Page(s)

Alford v. *United States*, 282 U.S. 687 (1931) 24, 25

Arizona v. *Fulminante*, 499 U.S. 279 (1991) 18

Bose Corp. v. *Consumers Union of United States, Inc.*, 466 U.S. 485 (1984) 19, 20

Brewer v. *Williams*, 430 U.S. 387 (1977) 19

Brinegar v. *United States*, 338 U.S. 160 (1949) 20

Browning-Ferris Industries of Vermont, Inc. v. *Kelco Disposal, Inc.*, 492 U.S. 257 (1989) 22

California v. *Green*, 399 U.S. 149 (1970) 21

Cooper Industries, Inc. v. *Leatherman Tool Group, Inc.*, 532 U.S. 424 (2001) 20, 22

Cooter & Gell v. *Hartmarx Corp.*, 496 U.S. 384 (1990) 18

Daubert v. *Merrell Dow Pharmaceuticals, Inc.*, 509 U.S. 579 (1993) 24

Davis v. *Alaska*, 415 U.S. 308 (1974) 10, 21, 25

Delaware v. *Van Arsdall*, 475 U.S. 673 (1986) 10, 22, 23

Derrick v. *Peterson*, 924 F.2d 813 (9th Cir. 1991) 19

Elcock v. *Kmart Corp.*, 233 F.3d 734 (3d Cir. 2000) 22

Geders v. *United States*, 425 U.S. 80 (1976) 24, 25

TABLE OF AUTHORITIES—Continued

Page(s)

General Electric Co. v. *Joiner*, 522 U.S. 136
  (1997) 23, 24

Glasser v. *United States*, 315 U.S. 60 (1942) 25, 26

Harte-Hanks Communications, Inc. v.
  Connaughton, 491 U.S. 657 (1989) 19

Ker v. *California*, 374 U.S. 23 (1963) 18

Kirby v. *United States*, 174 U.S. 47 (1899) 21

Lilly v. *Virginia*, 527 U.S. 116 (1999) 17, 18, 19

McNary v. *Haitian Refugee Center, Inc.*,
  498 U.S. 479 (1991) 21

Miller v. *Fenton*, 474 U.S. 104 (1985) 18, 20

Miranda v. *Arizona*, 384 U.S. 436 (1966) 18

News-Press v. *United States Department of
  Homeland Security*, 489 F.3d 1173
  (11th Cir. 2007) 15

Old Chief v. *United States*, 519 U.S. 172
  (1997) 24

Olden v. *Kentucky*, 488 U.S. 227 (1988) (per
  curiam) 8, 10

Ornelas v. *United States*, 517 U.S. 690
  (1996) 17, 18, 19, 20

Parker v. *Levy*, 417 U.S. 733 (1974) 16

Pierce v. *Underwood*, 487 U.S. 552 (1988) 18

Pointer v. *Texas*, 380 U.S. 400 (1965) 21

Pullman-Standard v. *Swint*, 456 U.S. 273
  (1982) 17, 18

TABLE OF AUTHORITIES—Continued

Page(s)

Salve Regina College v. *Russell*, 499 U.S. 225 (1991) 15, 18

Smith v. *Illinois*, 390 U.S. 129 (1968) 25

Spring Co. v. *Edgar*, 99 U.S. 645 (1879) 24

Strickland v. *Washington*, 466 U.S. 668 (1984) 18

Sumner v. *Mata*, 455 U.S. 591 (1982) 19

Thompson v. *Keohane*, 516 U.S. 99 (1995) 18

United States v. *Abel*, 469 U.S. 45 (1984) 24

United States v. *Allen*, 353 F. App'x 352 (11th Cir. 2009) 14

United States v. *Askanazi*, 14 F. App'x 538 (6th Cir. 2001) 14

United States v. *Ayala*, 43 M.J. 296 (C.A.A.F. 1995) 9, 13

United States v. *Bajakjian*, 524 U.S. 321 (1998) 17, 18

United States v. *Banker*, 60 M.J. 216 (C.A.A.F. 2004) 5

United States v. *Bentley*, 561 F.3d 803 (8th Cir. 2009) 12

United States v. *Buenaventura*, 45 M.J. 72 (C.A.A.F. 1996) 8

United States v. *Cain*, 59 M.J. 285 (C.A.A.F. 2004) 4

TABLE OF AUTHORITIES—Continued

Page(s)

United States v. Collier, 67 M.J. 347
(C.A.A.F. 2009) 8

United States v. Erving L., 147 F.3d 1240
(10th Cir. 1998) 19

United States v. Franco, 484 F.3d 347 (6th
Cir. 2007) 13

United States v. Frederick, 182 F.3d 496
(7th Cir. 1999) 17

United States v. Graham, 83 F.3d 1466
(D.C. Cir. 1996) 14

United States v. Hardy, 586 F.3d 1040 (6th
Cir. 2009) 14

United States v. Hooper, 26 C.M.R. 417
(C.M.A. 1958) 25

United States v. Israel, 60 M.J. 485
(C.A.A.F. 2005) 8

United States v. Jass, 569 F.3d 47 (2d Cir.
2009) 14

United States v. Jimenez, 464 F.3d 555 (5th
Cir. 2006) 12

United States v. Larson, 495 F.3d 1094 (9th
Cir. 2007) (en banc) 12, 13, 14, 23

United States v. LeBrun, 363 F.3d 715 (8th
Cir. 2004) (en banc) 19

United States v. McConney, 728 F.2d 1195
(9th Cir. 1984) (en banc) 17

TABLE OF AUTHORITIES—Continued

Page(s)

United States v. *McElhaney*, 54 M.J. 120
(C.A.A.F. 2000) 15

United States v. *Montelongo*, 420 F.3d 1169
(10th Cir. 2005) 12

United States v. *Moss*, 63 M.J. 233
(C.A.A.F. 2006) 8

United States v. *Mussare*, 450 F.3d 161 (3d
Cir. 2005) 22

United States v. *Nobles*, 422 U.S. 225 (1975) 26

United States v. *Orisnord*, 483 F.3d 1169
(11th Cir. 2007) 14

United States v. *Rosa*, 11 F.3d 315 (2d Cir.
1993) 13, 22

United States v. *Scheetz*, 293 F.3d 175 (4th
Cir. 2002) 13-14

United States v. *Schreane*, 331 F.3d 548
(6th Cir. 2003) 24

United States v. *Shaffer*, 46 M.J. 94
(C.A.A.F. 1997) 8

United States v. *Shelton*, 200 F. App'x 219
(4th Cir. 2006) 13

United States v. *Silveus*, 542 F.3d 993 (3d
Cir. 2008) 13

United States v. *Smith*, 308 F.3d 726 (7th
Cir. 2002) 12

United States v. *Vega Molina*, 407 F.3d 511
(1st Cir. 2005) 12

TABLE OF AUTHORITIES—Continued

Page(s)

United States v. *Vitale*, 459 F.3d 190 (2d Cir. 2006)..14

United States v. *Williams*, 504 U.S. 36 (1992)...16

United States v. *Williams*, 37 M.J. 352 (C.M.A. 1993)..24-25

Verizon Communications, Inc. v. *FCC*, 535 U.S. 467 (2002)...16

Weiss v. *United States*, 510 U.S. 163 (1994)..................4

Williams v. *Taylor*, 529 U.S. 362 (2000).......................19

CONSTITUTIONAL AND STATUTORY PROVISIONS

U.S. Const. amend VI..*passim*

8 U.S.C. § 1160(e)..21

10 U.S.C.
    § 818...4
    § 826...4
    § 832...3
    § 892...4

28 U.S.C.
    § 1259(3)..2
    § 2254(d)(1)...19

RULES

Federal Rule of Civil Procedure 11.................................18

TABLE OF AUTHORITIES—Continued

Page(s)

Federal Rule of Evidence
    403...24
    412...5
    702...24

Military Rule of Evidence 412 (2005 ed.) 5, 6

OTHER AUTHORITIES

Childress, Steven Alan & Martha S. Davis,
    Federal Standards of Review (3d ed. 1999)............15

Hamilton, Jesse, *Coast Guard Admiral Rep-*
    rimanded: Ex-Academy Superintendent
    To Retire After Probe Finds Inappropriate
    Behavior, Hartford Courant, Feb. 27, 2007,
    at A1 3-4

Kime, Patricia, *Academy Takes Heat Over Sex-*
    Assault Cases, Navy Times, Mar. 27, 2006,
    at 36 3

Lightman, David, *Academy Under Scrutiny;*
    Coast Guard Harassment Issue Gets At-
    tention of Congressional Panels, Hartford
    Courant, May 18, 2006, at B1 3

Yardley, William, *Coast Guard Addresses Sex*
    Assaults, N.Y. Times, Feb. 28, 2006, at B7 3

Blank Page

Supreme Court of the United States

No. 10-

WEBSTER M. SMITH,

Petitioner,

v.

UNITED STATES OF AMERICA,

Respondent.

ON PETITION FOR A WRIT OF CERTIORARI TO THE UNITED STATES COURT OF APPEALS FOR THE ARMED FORCES

PETITION FOR A WRIT OF CERTIORARI

Webster M. Smith respectfully petitions for a writ of certiorari to review the judgment of the United States Court of Appeals for the Armed Forces in this case.

OPINIONS BELOW

The opinion of the court of appeals (App. 1a-21a) is reported at 68 M.J. 445. The opinion of the intermediate appellate court, the Coast Guard Court of Criminal Appeals (App. 23a-58a), is reported at 66 M.J. 556. The order and opinion of the trial judge denying petitioner's request to conduct the cross-examination at issue here (App. 59a-64a) is unreported.

JURISDICTION

The judgment of the court of appeals was entered on March 29, 2010. This Court's jurisdiction is invoked under 28 U.S.C. § 1259(3).

CONSTITUTIONAL PROVISION INVOLVED

The Sixth Amendment to the United States Constitution provides in relevant part that "[i]n all criminal prosecutions, the accused shall enjoy the right ... to be confronted with the witnesses against him."

STATEMENT

This case implicates a deep circuit conflict regarding the standard of review that applies when a trial judge's restriction on the cross-examination of a prosecution witness is challenged on appeal as a violation of the Confrontation Clause. The Court of Appeals for the Armed Forces (CAAF) held here that the standard of review is abuse of discretion rather than de novo. Applying the former standard, the court rejected petitioner's Confrontation Clause claim by a vote of 3-2.

1. In early 2006, officials at the United States Coast Guard Academy filed sixteen specifications (the military equivalent of criminal charges) against petitioner Webster Smith, a cadet who was then a few months from graduation. *See* CAAF J.A. 89-92. Four weeks later, Academy officials lodged an additional five specifications. *Id.* at 93-95. Most of the specifications alleged that Mr. Smith had engaged in some form of sexual misconduct with one of several female cadets.[1]

---

[1] At the time these charges were brought, Academy officials, like their counterparts at the other service academies, were facing

Pursuant to Article 32 of the Uniform Code of Military Justice (UCMJ), 10 U.S.C. § 832, an investigation of the charges against Mr. Smith was conducted by an impartial officer. *See* CAAF J.A. 193-195. After completing his investigation (including hearing from all of the accusers), the investigating officer concluded that most of the charges lacked foundation. Specifically, he recommended that twelve of the twenty-one charges be dismissed outright, that two others be resolved administratively by Academy officials, and that just seven be referred for trial by general court-martial. *See* Appellate Ex. 17. As to nine of the twelve charges for which he recommended dismissal, the officer found that there were not even reasonable grounds to conclude that Mr. Smith had committed the offense. *See id.*

Disregarding several of the investigating officer's recommendations, the official overseeing the prosecution (the Academy superintendent) directed that eleven of the twenty-one charges be dismissed and that the other ten be tried by general court-martial. This was the first (and to date only) time in the Academy's 130-year history that a cadet had been court-martialed. *See, e.g.,* Jesse Hamilton, *Coast Guard Admiral Reprimanded: Ex-Academy Superintendent To Retire After Probe Finds Inappropriate Behavior,* Hartford

---

intense scrutiny and pressure from the public, the media, and Congress about perceived laxity in their handling of allegations of sexual harassment and sexual assault. *See, e.g.,* David Lightman, *Academy Under Scrutiny; Coast Guard Harassment Issue Gets Attention of Congressional Panels,* Hartford Courant, May 18, 2006, at B1; Patricia Kime, *Academy Takes Heat Over Sex-Assault Cases,* Navy Times, Mar. 27, 2006, at 36; William Yardley, *Coast Guard Addresses Sex Assaults,* N.Y. Times, Feb. 28, 2006, at B7.

Courant, Feb. 27, 2007, at A1. Mr. Smith pleaded not guilty to all ten charges.[2]

2. Prior to trial, the military judge (the military term for the trial judge, *see* 10 U.S.C. § 826) imposed a restriction on the defense's cross-examination of a key prosecution witness, SR.[3] SR, a fellow cadet, accused Mr. Smith of sexually assaulting her and extorting sexual favors from her. The defense maintained that the two cadets' sexual encounter was consensual and that SR was fabricating her accusations because the encounter occurred in Chase Hall, the Academy dormitory, where sexual activity is prohibited by cadet regulations and punishable by expulsion from the Academy, *see* App. 34a, 16a n.3. To support this argument, the defense intended to elicit on cross-examination the fact that SR had previously made a false allegation of sexual assault, telling Mr. Smith (and allowing him to tell others) that a consensual sexual encounter she had had with an enlisted man was not consensual.[4] Like the Chase Hall encounter, the encounter with the enlisted man was prohibited by cadet regulations (and hence the UCMJ, *see* 10 U.S.C. § 892; *see also United States* v. *Cain*, 59 M.J. 285, 292-293 (C.A.A.F. 2004)). The defense thus planned to argue to the jury ("members" in military parlance) that SR was once again falsely accus-

---

[2] The general court-martial had original jurisdiction under Article 18 of the UCMJ, 10 U.S.C. § 818. *See, e.g., Weiss* v. *United States*, 510 U.S. 163, 167 (1994).

[3] In their opinions in this case, the appellate courts referred to SR only by her initials. This petition does likewise.

[4] Mr. Smith testified at a pre-trial hearing that SR initially told him the encounter with the enlisted man was not consensual and later acknowledged that it was consensual. *See* App. 4a, 60a.

ing a man of assaulting her in order to evade discipline
that she could otherwise face for willingly engaging in
sexual activity that was barred by military regulations.
See App. 27a-28a, 40a, 62a-63a. Noting that the three
charges involving SR rested entirely on her testimony—the government offered no other evidence as to
any of them—the defense contended that Mr. Smith
was constitutionally entitled to inform the jury of facts
that bore so directly on her credibility. *See* CAAF J.A.
180-181.

The government sought to exclude the proposed
cross-examination of SR pursuant to Military Rule of
Evidence 412. *See* CAAF J.A. 183-187. That rule, the
nearly identical military counterpart to Federal Rule of
Evidence 412, generally bars the admission of
"[e]vidence offered to prove that any alleged victim engaged in other sexual behavior." M.R.E. 412(a)(1) (2005
ed.).[5] The rule includes an exception, however, for
"evidence the exclusion of which would violate the constitutional rights of the accused." M.R.E. 412(b)(1)(C).
This exception, which the defense invoked in seeking to
conduct the proposed cross-examination of SR, *see*
CAAF J.A. 180-181, "addresses an accused's Sixth
Amendment right of confrontation," *United States* v.
Banker, 60 M.J. 216, 221 (C.A.A.F. 2004). Hence, the
issue for the military judge was whether the Confrontation Clause required that the proposed cross-
examination be allowed.

The judge concluded that it did not. *See* App. 59a-
64a. He agreed that the defense's theory about SR's

---

[5] Minor amendments were made to Military Rule of Evidence
412 in 2008. The version cited herein is the one that was in effect
throughout the court-martial proceedings.

prior fabrication of assault "would be a valid reason for admitting this evidence under M.R.E. 412(b)(1)(C)," i.e., pursuant to Mr. Smith's Sixth Amendment rights. App. 63a. He nonetheless prohibited the proposed cross-examination, in part because allowing it could, he believed, "sidetrack[] the member[s'] attention to a collateral issue," App. 64a, and in part because the only evidence of SR's prior false accusation came from Mr. Smith, whose credibility the judge questioned, *see* App. 63a.[6] The judge ultimately allowed defense counsel to reveal to the jury only that SR had lied to Mr. Smith in unspecified ways about unspecified conduct that she believed involved a violation of cadet regulations and possibly the UCMJ (but for which prosecutors had indicated they would not prosecute her). *See* App. 4a-5a, 19a & n.6; CAAF J.A. 145, 148-149.

3. Following a week-long trial, the jury acquitted Mr. Smith on six of the ten charges. *See* CAAF J.A. 173-174. It convicted on the other four, as well as on a lesser-included offense of one of the six counts of acquittal. *See id.*; App. 2a. The three convictions that pertained to sexual conduct (sodomy, indecent assault, and extortion of sexual favors) were all based on the allegations by SR, whose credibility—including motive to lie—the defense was not permitted to explore fully.

---

[6] SR, the only other apparent source of evidence on the point, invoked her privilege against self-incrimination and thus did not testify at the pre-trial hearing on the proposed cross-examination. *See* App. 4a, 54a, 59a; CAAF J.A. 177-178. Although she dropped that invocation in order to testify at trial, the military judge did not require her, upon waiving the privilege, to address whether in fact she had made a prior false accusation so that he could revisit his ruling on the proposed cross-examination in the event she corroborated Mr. Smith's testimony by admitting that she had.

By contrast, the jury acquitted Mr. Smith of every sex-related charge on which his accuser was subject to full cross-examination. The verdict also meant that the government had failed to prove even one of the original sex-related charges that Academy officials had leveled against Mr. Smith. All of those charges were either dismissed before trial (many as lacking any foundation, *see supra* p.3) or resulted in acquittal.

The jury sentenced Mr. Smith to six months' confinement, forfeiture of all pay and allowances, and dismissal from the Coast Guard (i.e., expulsion from the Academy). *See* App. 2a; CAAF J.A. 175. Mr. Smith served his period of confinement immediately after trial, earning release a month early for good behavior.[7]

4. After the Coast Guard Court of Criminal Appeals affirmed his convictions and sentence—over a lengthy dissent regarding the restriction on the cross-examination of SR, *see* App. 40a-58a—Mr. Smith petitioned CAAF for further review. CAAF granted review of the Sixth Amendment question, but following briefing and argument it affirmed by a splintered 3-2 vote. *See* App. 1a-21a.

In presenting his Confrontation Clause claim, Mr. Smith argued that because he was raising a constitutional challenge to the military judge's ruling, CAAF should review the ruling de novo rather than for abuse of discretion. In support of that argument, Mr. Smith

---

[7] Following his release, Mr. Smith returned to his home state of Texas, where he has completed his undergraduate work, married, become a father, and remained steadily employed. Upon his return, however, Mr. Smith was also forced to register as a sex offender, as Texas law mandates lifelong registration for indecent-assault convictions.

cited cases from several circuits that employ de novo
review of Confrontation Clause claims like his. Writing
for a two-judge plurality, Judge Stucky rejected that
position, holding that under CAAF precedent, review
was only for abuse of discretion. *See* App. 5a (citing
United States v. *Moss*, 63 M.J. 233, 236 (C.A.A.F. 2006),
and *United States* v. *Israel*, 60 M.J. 485, 488 (C.A.A.F.
2005)).[8]

Applying that standard, the plurality concluded
that "[t]he military judge did not abuse his discretion."
App. 7a. The plurality deemed it significant that the
defense had been allowed to show the jury that SR had
lied to Mr. Smith about conduct that she believed could
have threatened her career. *See id.* The plurality also
reasoned that "[w]hile Cadet SR's credibility was in
contention, it is unclear why the lurid nuances of her
sexual past would have added much to Appellant's extant theory of fabrication." *Id.* Finally, the plurality
sought to distinguish cases cited by Mr. Smith, including this Court's decision in *Olden* v. *Kentucky*, 488 U.S.
227 (1988) (per curiam), that held comparable restrictions on the cross-examination of key prosecution witnesses to be unconstitutional. *See* App. 7a-8a; *see also*
App. 29a-31a (court of criminal appeals majority seeking to distinguish other CAAF cases with similar holdings).

Judge Baker, also applying the abuse-of-discretion
standard, concurred in the result. *See* App. 8a-10a. He

---

[8] CAAF has long applied this standard to Confrontation
Clause claims. *See, e.g., United States* v. *Collier*, 67 M.J. 347, 353
(C.A.A.F. 2009); *United States* v. *Shaffer*, 46 M.J. 94, 98 (C.A.A.F.
1997); *United States* v. *Buenaventura*, 45 M.J. 72, 79 (C.A.A.F.
1996).

acknowledged that the military judge's ruling might well have violated the Confrontation Clause on the theory that the jury "needed to know the nature of 'the secret' in order to assess beyond a reasonable doubt whether SR might succumb to pressure to protect the secret." App. 9a. But in his view, Mr. Smith's alternate "theory of admission [wa]s too far-fetched to pass constitutional ... muster." *Id.*[9]

Judge Erdmann, joined by Chief Judge Effron, agreed that CAAF "review[s] a military judge's decision to admit or exclude evidence for an abuse of discretion." App. 13a (citing *United States* v. *Ayala*, 43 M.J. 296, 298 (C.A.A.F. 1995)). But they dissented from the other judges' application of that standard. *See* App. 10a-21a. The fatal problem in their view was that "the military judge prevented the defense from presenting to the panel an explanation of the circumstances that would have provided the complainant to make a false allegation of" sexual assault. App. 10a; *see also* App. 21a ("Smith had a commonsense explanation

---

[9] Two of Judge Baker's articulated bases for this conclusion were factually incorrect. First, Judge Baker stated that "it was SR herself who reported her sexual contact with Appellant; this cuts against Appellant's theory that SR would lie to conceal her own misconduct." App. 9a. In fact, "[t]he record does not disclose whether SR voluntarily came forward or was first approached by" Coast Guard investigators. App. 52a n.8 (court of criminal appeals dissent); *see also* App. 51a-53a. Second, Judge Baker stated that "to support [Mr. Smith's] theory of admission the members needed to know that SR had 'lied' to Appellant about her sexual misconduct," and "[t]his much the military judge permitted." App. 9a. To the contrary, the military judge did not permit the jury to hear that what "SR had 'lied' to Appellant about [was] sexual misconduct." *Id.* Indeed, that prohibition was the crux of Mr. Smith's challenge on appeal.

for SR's claim that the sexual activity was nonconsensual and the military judge's ruling prevented the members from considering this theory."). Emphasizing that "this was a 'he said-she said' case and for the charges at issue in this appeal, the critical question for the members was the credibility of the sole prosecution witness," App. 17a (footnote omitted), the dissenters concluded—relying on this Court's precedent—that a Sixth Amendment violation had occurred because "'[a] reasonable jury might have received a significantly different impression of [the witness's] credibility had [defense counsel] been permitted to pursue his proposed line of cross-examination,'" App. 14a-15a (alterations in original) (quoting *Delaware* v. *Van Arsdall*, 475 U.S. 673, 680 (1986)); *accord* App. 41a (court of criminal appeals dissent) ("The excessive restrictions imposed on Appellant's Sixth Amendment confrontation rights allowed SR to testify through non-factual euphemisms on critical issues related to the Government's proof and her own credibility, and allowed the Government to create a substantially different impression of her truthfulness than what the defense had sought to show through the excluded evidence.").

The dissenters also disagreed with the plurality that the cross-examination allowed by the military judge was sufficient, explaining that "[w]ith this limited information about SR's secret, the members were left to speculate whether the secret was a minor disciplinary infraction or a more serious charge, but they had no idea that the proffered evidence directly implicated SR's motive and credibility." App. 19a-20a; *see also* App. 45a-46a (court of criminal appeals dissent) (citing *Davis* v. *Alaska*, 415 U.S. 308, 316-317 (1974), and *Olden*, 488 U.S. at 232 (per curiam)). As to the plurality's stated doubt about the need for the "lurid nuances" of SR's secret, App. 7a, the dissenters explained that what was important about the proposed cross-examination, and what its focus would have been, was "not the lurid nuances of the victim's sexual past ..., but rather the allegation that SR had previously lied about a sexual encounter under similar circumstances." App. 18a (internal quotation marks omitted).[10]

REASONS FOR GRANTING THE PETITION

CAAF's holding regarding the appropriate standard for appellate review of Confrontation Clause claims like Mr. Smith's conflicts with the holdings of several other courts of appeals. The conflict is established and the issue is both recurring and important. Moreover, this case is a good vehicle for resolving the conflict, both because the issue was raised throughout the case and because CAAF's splintered decision applying abuse-of-discretion review shows that the use of that relatively lax standard may well have determined the outcome here. Finally, CAAF's use of an abuse-of-discretion standard is wrong, as Mr. Smith had a right to plenary appellate review of his constitutional claim raising a mixed question of law and fact. Under these circumstances, this Court's review is warranted.

---

[10] In addition to defending the merits of the military judge's ruling, the government raised a jurisdictional objection before CAAF, contending that Mr. Smith's petition for discretionary review by that court was untimely. CAAF unanimously rejected that argument. *See* App. 2a-3a (plurality opinion), 10a (dissent), 8a-10a (Baker, J., concurring in the result) (implicitly rejecting the jurisdictional argument by addressing the merits).

I. CAAF's Standard-Of-Review Holding Implicates An Established Circuit Conflict On An Important And Recurring Question Of Federal Law

A. The Courts Of Appeals Are Deeply Divided Over What Standard Of Review Applies To Confrontation Clause Claims Like Mr. Smith's

CAAF employed abuse-of-discretion review in resolving Mr. Smith's Sixth Amendment challenge to the military judge's restriction on the defense's cross-examination of SR. *See, e.g.*, App. 5a. That approach conflicts with the holdings of five circuits, which consider comparable Confrontation Clause claims de novo, reserving abuse-of-discretion review for non-constitutional challenges. For example, the Seventh Circuit has stated that "[o]rdinarily, a district court's evidentiary rulings are reviewed for abuse of discretion. However, when the restriction [on cross-examination] implicates the criminal defendant's Sixth Amendment right to confront witnesses against him, ... the standard of review becomes de novo." *United States* v. *Smith*, 308 F.3d 726, 738 (7th Cir. 2002) (citation omitted). The First, Fifth, Eighth, and Tenth Circuits have adopted the same approach. *See, e.g.*, *United States* v. *Vega Molina*, 407 F.3d 511, 522 (1st Cir. 2005); *United States* v. *Jimenez*, 464 F.3d 555, 558-559 (5th Cir. 2006); *United States* v. *Bentley*, 561 F.3d 803, 808 (8th Cir. 2009), *cert. denied*, 130 S. Ct. 1275 (2009); *United States* v. *Montelongo*, 420 F.3d 1169, 1173 (10th Cir. 2005).[11]

---

[11] In *United States* v. *Larson*, 495 F.3d 1094 (9th Cir. 2007) (en banc), the Ninth Circuit stated that it was adopting an approach that "br[ought it] in line with [these five] sister circuits,"

13

Six other circuits, by contrast—the Second, Third, Fourth, Sixth, Eleventh, and District of Columbia Circuits—take the same approach that CAAF does, applying abuse-of-discretion review even when a restriction on the cross-examination of a prosecution witness is attacked on constitutional grounds.[12] The Sixth Circuit, for example, stated in one case that "[defendant] argues that his right to confrontation was violated when the trial court 'unfairly' limited his cross-examination of [a] government witness .... We review the district court's restriction on a defendant's right to cross-examine witnesses for abuse of discretion." *United States* v. *Franco*, 484 F.3d 347, 353 (6th Cir. 2007). Cases from the other circuits in this group are to the same effect. *See, e.g., United States* v. *Rosa*, 11 F.3d 315, 335 (2d Cir. 1993); *United States* v. *Silveus*, 542 F.3d 993, 1005 (3d Cir. 2008); *United States* v. *Shelton*, 200 F. App'x 219, 221 (4th Cir. 2006) (citing *United States* v. *Scheetz*,

---

id. at 1101 n.6 (citing a case from each of the five). The court's actual holding, however, was that abuse-of-discretion review is proper for some constitutional challenges, specifically those addressing "a limitation on the scope of questioning within a given area" rather than "the exclusion of an [entire] area of inquiry." *Id.* at 1101.

[12] The dissenters stated in this case that under the abuse-of-discretion standard, conclusions of law are reviewed de novo. App. 13a. The authority they cited for that statement, however, *United States* v. *Ayala*, involved a suppression ruling rather than a restriction on cross-examination. *See* 43 M.J. at 298. To petitioner's knowledge, no CAAF case states that the abuse-of-discretion standard repeatedly applied by the court when reviewing restrictions on defendants' cross-examination includes de novo review of legal conclusions. Nor did the plurality or the concurring judge here indicate that any aspect of their review was conducted de novo.

293 F.3d 175, 184 (4th Cir. 2002)); *United States* v. *Oris-nord*, 483 F.3d 1169, 1178 (11th Cir. 2007); *United States* v. *Graham*, 83 F.3d 1466, 1474 (D.C. Cir. 1996).[13]

In short, CAAF's use of an abuse-of-discretion standard in this case perpetuates a clear—and recognized—conflict in the circuits. *See United States* v. *Larson*, 495 F.3d 1094, 1100 & n.5 (9th Cir. 2007) (en banc) (resolving "an intra-circuit conflict regarding the standard of review for Confrontation Clause challenges to a trial court's limitations on cross-examination" while acknowledging a parallel "disagreement among the circuits").

B. The Question Presented Is Recurring And Important, And This Case Is A Good Vehicle For Deciding It

The circuit conflict at issue here warrants resolution by this Court. As indicated by the cases cited in the previous section, the constitutionality of restrictions on cross-examination arises frequently in criminal

---

[13] A few unpublished decisions from some of the circuits in this group have reviewed restrictions on cross-examination de novo, notwithstanding (and without acknowledging) the contrary precedent cited in the text. *See, e.g., United States* v. *Allen*, 353 F. App'x 352, 354 (11th Cir. 2009) (per curiam); *United States* v. *Askanazi*, 14 F. App'x 538, 540 (6th Cir. 2001) (per curiam). Other cases, addressing other types of Confrontation Clause claims, have proclaimed in dicta that all such claims are subject to de novo review—again without confronting the cases cited in the text. *See, e.g., United States* v. *Jass*, 569 F.3d 47, 55 (2d Cir. 2009) (*Bruton* claim: "We review '[a]lleged violations of the Confrontation Clause ... de novo[.]'" (alteration and omission in original) (quoting *United States* v. *Vitale*, 459 F.3d 190, 195 (2d Cir. 2006))), *cert. denied*, 130 S. Ct. 2128 (2010); *United States* v. *Hardy*, 586 F.3d 1040, 1043 (6th Cir. 2009) (similar for admission of affidavit).

prosecutions, and in every part of the country. Those cases also show that the conflict over the standard for appellate review of such restrictions is established; there is thus no benefit to be gained by giving the lower courts additional time to consider the issue. Moreover, the question presented is important, because the standard of review can determine the outcome of an appeal. *See Salve Regina Coll.* v. *Russell*, 499 U.S. 225, 238 (1991) ("[T]he difference between a rule of deference and the duty to exercise independent review is much more than a mere matter of degree." (internal quotation marks omitted)); *see also, e.g., News-Press* v. *United States Dep't of Homeland Sec.*, 489 F.3d 1173, 1187 (11th Cir. 2007) ("In even moderately close cases, the standard of review may be dispositive of an appellate court's decision."); 1 Steven Alan Childress & Martha S. Davis, *Federal Standards of Review* § 1.02, at 1-16 (3d ed. 1999). That is particularly true when one standard is highly deferential: CAAF, for example, has stated that "the abuse of discretion standard is a strict one," satisfied only when "[t]he challenged action [is] arbitrary, fanciful, clearly unreasonable, or clearly erroneous," *United States* v. *McElhaney*, 54 M.J. 120, 130 (C.A.A.F. 2000) (internal quotation marks omitted). Finally, disuniformity created by the conflict directly affects a fundamental individual right. Some defendants in criminal cases enjoy less protection of the critical right to confront their accusers because of the fortuity of where their trials were held—or, as to cases decided by CAAF, because they have chosen to wear the nation's uniform.

This case presents a good vehicle to resolve the circuit conflict. To begin with, Mr. Smith's standard-of-review argument was both pressed and passed upon in the court of appeals, *see* Pet'r's CAAF Br. 12-13; App.

5a, rendering the issue suitable for review by certiorari. *See, e.g., Verizon Commc'ns, Inc.* v. *FCC*, 535 U.S. 467, 530 (2002) (quoting *United States* v. *Williams*, 504 U.S. 36, 41 (1992)). In addition, CAAF's rejection of Mr. Smith's argument may well have determined the ultimate outcome. Even applying highly deferential review, CAAF was narrowly divided as to the constitutionality of the military judge's ruling in this case. If even one of the three judges who deemed that ruling not to be an abuse of discretion were to conclude, upon reviewing without deference, that it was inconsistent with the Sixth Amendment, Mr. Smith would prevail.[14]

II. CAAF's Standard-Of-Review Holding Is Wrong

This Court's review is also warranted because CAAF's use of an abuse-of-discretion standard to review Mr. Smith's Confrontation Clause claim was erroneous. The military judge's ruling that Mr. Smith challenged presented a mixed question of law and fact. When a constitutional right is involved, as here, this Court has repeatedly held de novo review of such mixed questions appropriate. The decisions from this Court that CAAF and other courts have relied on to justify abuse-of-discretion review are inapposite.

---

[14] The military context in which this case arises does not affect its suitability as a vehicle to answer the question presented. Although servicemembers' constitutional rights can be more circumscribed than those of their civilian counterparts when morale, good order and discipline, or other military interests so require, *see Parker* v. *Levy*, 417 U.S. 733, 758 (1974), that is not the case here. CAAF has never articulated a military-specific rationale for employing abuse-of-discretion review in cases like this (nor did the government offer one below), and in fact no military interest would be undermined if CAAF reviewed constitutional challenges to restrictions on defendants' cross-examination without deference.

A. Under This Court's Precedent, Mixed Questions Of Law And Fact Are Reviewed De Novo When Constitutional Rights Are Involved

The military judge's restriction on the cross-examination of SR involved a quintessential "mixed question[] of law and fact—*i.e.*, [a] question[] in which the historical facts are admitted or established, the rule of law is undisputed, and the issue is whether the facts satisfy the ... standard." *Pullman-Standard* v. *Swint*, 456 U.S. 273, 289 n.19 (1982). Under this Court's cases, such questions are reviewed de novo when, as here, they implicate constitutional rights. As a plurality explained in *Lilly* v. *Virginia*, 527 U.S. 116 (1999), the Court's "prior opinions ... indicate that ... with ... fact-intensive, mixed questions of constitutional law, ... '[i]ndependent review is ... necessary ... to maintain control of, and to clarify, the legal principles' governing the factual circumstances necessary to satisfy the protections of the Bill of Rights," *id.* at 136 (alteration and last two omissions in original) (quoting *Ornelas* v. *United States*, 517 U.S. 690, 697 (1996)); *see also United States* v. *Bajakjian*, 524 U.S. 321, 337 n.10 (1998) (employing de novo review because the pertinent issue "calls for the application of a constitutional standard to the facts of a particular case"); *Pullman-Standard*, 456 U.S. at 290 n.19 ("There is also support in decisions of this Court for the proposition that conclusions on mixed questions of law and fact are independently reviewable by an appellate court." (citations omitted)); *United States* v. *Frederick*, 182 F.3d 496, 499 (7th Cir. 1999) (Posner, J.) (noting that this Court has embraced de novo review of mixed questions involving "certain constitutional issues"); *United States* v. *McConney*, 728 F.2d 1195, 1203 (9th Cir. 1984) (en banc) ("The predominance of factors favoring de novo review is even more striking when the mixed question implicates constitutional rights." (citing *Ker* v. *California*, 374 U.S. 23 (1963))).[15]

The Court has thus held that de novo review—though with deference typically given to associated factual findings—is appropriate for a wide variety of trial court rulings that implicate constitutional rights. These include rulings on: whether a hearsay statement bears sufficient indicia of "trustworthiness" to satisfy the Confrontation Clause, *see Lilly*, 527 U.S. at 136 (plurality opinion); whether a fine is unconstitutionally excessive, *see Bajakjian*, 524 U.S. at 336 n.10; whether police had probable cause or reasonable suspicion to conduct a search, *see Ornelas*, 517 U.S. at 699; whether a defendant was "in custody" for purposes of *Miranda* v. *Arizona*, 384 U.S. 436 (1966), *see Thompson* v. *Keohane*, 516 U.S. 99, 112-113 (1995); whether a confession was voluntary, *see Arizona* v. *Fulminante*, 499 U.S. 279, 287 (1991) (citing *Miller* v. *Fenton*, 474 U.S. 104, 110 (1985)); whether defense counsel was constitutionally ineffective, *see Strickland* v. *Washington*, 466 U.S. 668, 698 (1984); whether a pre-trial identification proce-

---

[15] Where constitutional rights are not implicated, "deferential review of mixed questions of law and fact is warranted when it appears that the district court is 'better positioned' than the appellate court to decide the issue in question or that probing appellate scrutiny will not contribute to the clarity of legal doctrine." *Salve Regina Coll.*, 499 U.S. at 233; *see also Cooter & Gell* v. *Hartmarx Corp.*, 496 U.S. 384, 405 (1990) (adopting deferential review of rulings under Federal Rule of Civil Procedure 11); *Pierce* v. *Underwood*, 487 U.S. 552, 558 n.1 (1988) (citing other examples); *Pullman-Standard*, 456 U.S. at 290 n.19 (citing examples of both approaches).

dure was unconstitutionally suggestive, *see Sumner* v. *Mata*, 455 U.S. 591, 597 (1982) (per curiam); whether a defendant waived his right to counsel, *see Brewer* v. *Williams*, 430 U.S. 387, 403-404 (1977); and several First Amendment questions, *see Harte-Hanks Commc'ns, Inc.* v. *Connaughton*, 491 U.S. 657, 685-686 n.33 (1989) (citing cases).[16]

The Court's rationale for these various holdings supports de novo review here. *First,* the Court has repeatedly observed in these cases that "the [relevant] legal rules ... acquire content only through application. Independent review is therefore necessary if appellate courts are to maintain control of, and to clarify, the le-

---

[16] Although some of these cases involved review of state-court judgments, their standard-of-review holdings apply equally to federal cases like this one. *See Lilly*, 527 U.S. at 136 (plurality opinion) (relying on *Ornelas*, a federal criminal case, to support its standard-of-review holding in a state criminal case); *see also Bose Corp.* v. *Consumers Union of U.S., Inc.*, 466 U.S. 485, 499 (1984) ("[S]urely it would pervert the concept of federalism for this Court to lay claim to a broader power of review over state-court judgments than it exercises in reviewing the judgments of intermediate federal courts."). That is true even for decisions from this Court on federal habeas review of a state-court judgment. While those cases' standard-of-review holdings generally do not apply in the habeas context post-AEDPA, *see Williams* v. *Taylor*, 529 U.S. 362, 411 (2000) (citing 28 U.S.C. § 2254(d)(1)), they remain valid and instructive for cases on direct review (state or federal). *See Ornelas*, 517 U.S. at 697 (citing *Miller*, a state-habeas case, to support its standard-of-review holding in a direct-review case); *see also, e.g., United States* v. *LeBrun*, 363 F.3d 715, 719 (8th Cir. 2004) (en banc) ("*Thompson's* rationale [in the habeas context] requires that on direct appeal we review the district court's custody determination de novo."); *United States* v. *Erving L.*, 147 F.3d 1240, 1245 (10th Cir. 1998) (similar, citing *Derrick* v. *Peterson*, 924 F.2d 813, 818 (9th Cir. 1991)).

gal principles." *Ornelas*, 517 U.S. at 697, *quoted in, e.g.,*
Cooper Indus., Inc. v. *Leatherman Tool Group, Inc.*,
532 U.S. 424, 436 (2001); *accord Miller*, 474 U.S. at 114.
The same is true of the Sixth Amendment "rules" that
apply to restrictions on the cross-examination of prosecution witnesses. *Second*, the Court has stated in the
search-and-seizure context that a

> policy of sweeping deference would permit, "[i]n
> the absence of any significant difference in the
> facts," "the Fourth Amendment's incidence [to]
> tur[n] on whether different trial judges draw
> general conclusions that the facts are sufficient
> or insufficient to constitute probable cause."
> Such varied results would be inconsistent with
> the idea of a unitary system of law.

Ornelas, 517 U.S. at 697 (alterations in original) (quoting *Brinegar* v. *United States*, 338 U.S. 160, 171 (1949)).
Again, the same is true as to the Confrontation Clause.

More generally, this Court has explained that plenary appellate review of constitutional mixed questions
"reflects a deeply held conviction that judges—and particularly Members of this Court—must exercise such
review in order to preserve the precious liberties established and ordained by the Constitution." *Bose
Corp.* v. *Consumers Union of U.S., Inc.*, 466 U.S. 485,
510-511 (1984); *see also id.* at 503 ("When the standard
governing the decision of a particular case is provided
by the Constitution, this Court's role in marking out
the limits of the standard through the process of case-
by-case adjudication is of special importance."). That is
surely true of a defendant's right to confront the witnesses against him through cross-examination: This
Court has labeled cross-examination "the greatest legal
engine ever invented for the discovery of truth."

California v. *Green*, 399 U.S. 149, 158 (1970) (internal quotation marks omitted). It has also deemed the right of confrontation to be "one of the fundamental guarantees of life and liberty," *Kirby* v. *United States*, 174 U.S. 47, 55 (1899), and so "fundamental and essential to a fair trial" as to be incorporated against the States, *Pointer* v. *Texas*, 380 U.S. 400, 403 (1965). And it has stated that an impermissible restriction on a defendant's right of cross-examination is "constitutional error of the first magnitude." *Davis* v. *Alaska*, 415 U.S. 308, 318 (1974). Deferential review of trial-court rulings is insufficient to safeguard such a critical constitutional right.[17]

Finally, this Court's cases support the specific approach espoused by Mr. Smith and adopted by several circuits, whereby non-constitutional challenges to restrictions on cross-examination are reviewed for abuse of discretion while constitutional challenges are reviewed de novo. In *Cooper Industries, Inc.* v. *Leatherman Tool Group, Inc.*, the Court adopted the same approach for punitive damages awards. "If no constitutional issue is raised" regarding the excessiveness of such an award, the Court stated, "the role of the appel-

---

[17] Decisions outside the mixed-question context reinforce the conclusion that de novo review is appropriate here. For example, in *McNary* v. *Haitian Refugee Center, Inc.*, 498 U.S. 479 (1991), this Court construed a statutory provision mandating abuse-of-discretion review of certain individual immigration decisions. *See id.* at 485-486 & n.6 (discussing 8 U.S.C. § 1160(e)). The Court held that the statute did not preclude judicial review of due process challenges to the broader immigration program—and part of its rationale was that "the abuse-of-discretion standard ... does not apply to constitutional or statutory claims, which are reviewed *de novo* by the courts." *Id.* at 493.

late court ... is merely to review the trial court's [excessiveness] 'determination under an abuse-of-discretion standard.'" 532 U.S. at 433 (quoting *Browning-Ferris Indus. of Vt., Inc.* v. *Kelco Disposal, Inc.*, 492 U.S. 257, 279 (1989)). By contrast, the Court went on to hold (relying on *Ornelas* and *Bajakajian*), "courts of appeals should apply a *de novo* standard of review when passing on ... the constitutionality of punitive damages awards." *Id.* at 436.

What all these cases recognize is the anomaly of employing an abuse-of-discretion standard when the issue is whether or not a particular ruling violated a constitutional right. Such a standard suggests that a district court has "discretion" to commit a constitutional violation, and that appellate judges could uphold a ruling even if they believe that such a violation occurred. *See, e.g., Elcock* v. *Kmart Corp.*, 233 F.3d 734, 743 (3d Cir. 2000) ("Of course, an abuse of discretion means much more than that the appellate court disagrees with the trial court."). That is plainly wrong.

B. The Cases Relied On By Courts That Employ Abuse-Of-Discretion Review Do Not Support That Approach

The circuits that have reviewed Confrontation Clause challenges to restrictions on cross-examination deferentially have not addressed the cases discussed in the previous section. They have instead relied on other decisions by this Court that supposedly endorse abuse-of-discretion review. That reliance is misplaced.

To begin with, several circuits have based their choice of deferential review on language in *Delaware* v. *Van Arsdall*, 475 U.S. 673 (1986). *See, e.g., Rosa*, 11 F.3d at 335; *United States* v. *Mussare*, 450 F.3d 161, 169 (3d Cir. 2005). But what the Court said in the relevant portion of *Van Arsdall* is that "trial judges retain wide latitude insofar as the Confrontation Clause is concerned to impose reasonable limits on ... cross-examination based on concerns about, among other things, harassment, prejudice, confusion of the issues, the witness' safety, or interrogation that is repetitive or only marginally relevant." 475 U.S. at 679. That statement reveals nothing about the proper appellate standard of review. It instead addresses the substance of the Confrontation Clause, and in particular it rejects the notion that that clause, as a substantive matter, proscribes any restrictions on defendants' cross-examination. This is clear from the immediately preceding sentence, in which the Court stated that "[i]t does not follow, of course, that the Confrontation Clause of the Sixth Amendment prevents a trial judge from imposing any limits on defense counsel's inquiry into the potential bias of a prosecution witness." *Id.* It is also clear from the next few paragraphs, where the Court went on to find that a Confrontation Clause violation had occurred—without ever referring to abuse of discretion. *See id.* at 679-680.[18]

The Sixth Circuit has also relied on this Court's statement in *General Electric Co.* v. *Joiner*, 522 U.S. 136, 141 (1997), that "abuse of discretion is the proper

---

[18] The Ninth Circuit similarly relied on *Van Arsdall* in holding that the standard of review depends on the details of the defendant's Confrontation Clause challenge, i.e., that de novo review applies when the trial court "exclu[des] ... an [entire] area of inquiry," but not when it limits "the scope of questioning within a given area." *Larson*, 495 F.3d at 1101. As just discussed, however, *Van Arsdall* addressed only the substance of the confrontation guarantee. The Ninth Circuit's holding, moreover, improperly conflates substance with the standard of review.

standard of review of a district court's evidentiary rulings." *See United States* v. *Schreane*, 331 F.3d 548, 564 (6th Cir. 2003) (citing *Joiner* for the proposition that "[a]n appellate court reviews all evidentiary rulings—including constitutional challenges to evidentiary rulings—under the abuse-of-discretion standard"). *Joiner* was not a criminal case, however, and thus did not implicate the Confrontation Clause. Moreover, the relevant ruling in *Joiner* was not a constitutional one but rather a ruling on the exclusion of expert testimony under Federal Rule of Evidence 702 and *Daubert* v. *Merrell Dow Pharmaceuticals, Inc.*, 509 U.S. 579 (1993). *See Joiner*, 522 U.S. at 138-139. The same is true of the cases *Joiner* cited to support its statement that evidentiary rulings are reviewed for abuse of discretion; each likewise concerned a non-constitutional ruling by the trial judge. *See Old Chief* v. *United States*, 519 U.S. 172, 180 (1997) (balancing under Federal Rule of Evidence 403 in regard to admission of defendant's prior conviction); *United States* v. *Abel*, 469 U.S. 45, 54-55 (1984) (same in regard to admission of government rebuttal testimony); *Spring Co.* v. *Edgar*, 99 U.S. 645, 658 (1879) (admission of expert testimony). In light of the mixed-question precedent from this Court discussed in the previous section, *Joiner*'s reference to "evidentiary rulings" is most sensibly read to refer only to non-constitutional rulings. *Joiner* is thus consistent with Mr. Smith's contention that non-constitutional challenges to restrictions on cross-examination should be reviewed for abuse of discretion while constitutional claims should be reviewed de novo.

CAAF's deferential review in cases like this, meanwhile, traces to *Geders* v. *United States*, 425 U.S. 80 (1976), and *Alford* v. *United States*, 282 U.S. 687 (1931). *See, e.g., United States* v. *Williams*, 37 M.J. 352, 361

(C.M.A. 1993) (citing *Geders*); *United States* v. *Hooper*, 26 C.M.R. 417, 426 (C.M.A. 1958) (citing *Alford*). Neither case supports deferential review of constitutional challenges. The Court in *Alford* did review a restriction on cross-examination for abuse of discretion, *see* 282 U.S. at 694, but nothing in its opinion indicates that the defendant's attack on the restriction was constitutionally based. Indeed, the opinion never mentions either the Sixth Amendment generally or the Confrontation Clause in particular. Not until decades later did this Court state that *Alford*'s holding included a "constitutional dimension," *Davis*, 415 U.S. at 318 n.6 (citing *Smith* v. *Illinois*, 390 U.S. 129, 132-133 (1968))—and in doing so it plainly recognized the inconsistency between that "constitutional dimension" and *Alford*'s use of abuse-of-discretion review, *see id.* ("*Although* ... we reversed [in *Alford*] because of abuse of discretion and prejudicial error, the constitutional dimension of our holding in *Alford* is not in doubt." (emphasis added)).

Geders provides even less support for CAAF's use of deferential review. The Court in *Geders* did not review a restriction on cross-examination, nor say that such restrictions are reviewed for abuse of discretion. It stated that a trial judge's determination regarding "the order in which parties will adduce proof"—a nonconstitutional matter—"will be reviewed only for abuse of discretion." 425 U.S. at 86. In the next sentence the Court, citing *Glasser* v. *United States*, 315 U.S. 60, 83 (1942), noted that, "[w]ithin limits, the judge may ... control the scope of examination of witnesses," *Geders*, 425 U.S. at 86-87. But while *Glasser* did review a restriction on cross-examination for abuse of discretion, as with *Alford* there is no indication in *Glasser* (the relevant portion of which totals only three sentences) that the defendant had raised a constitutional challenge.

See Glasser, 315 U.S. at 83.[19] Again, then, this Court's precedent is consistent with the approach used by five courts of appeals and urged by Mr. Smith here. In any event, to the extent these cases reflect any uncertainty on the question presented, that is an additional factor weighing in favor of review.

CONCLUSION

The petition for a writ of certiorari should be granted.

Respectfully submitted.

DANIEL S. VOLCHOK
Counsel of Record
SETH P. WAXMAN
A. STEPHEN HUT, JR.
EDWARD C. DUMONT
WILMER CUTLER PICKERING
  HALE AND DORR LLP
1875 Pennsylvania Avenue N.W.
Washington, D.C. 20006
(202) 663-6000
daniel.volchok@wilmerhale.com

JUNE 2010

---

[19] The Court in *Geders* also cited *United States* v. *Nobles*, 422 U.S. 225 (1975), but *Nobles* did not involve the Confrontation Clause. The issue there was whether the defense had to disclose certain material in order to permit adequate cross-examination by the *prosecution*. *See Nobles*, 422 U.S. at 227; *see also id.* at 241 (labeling the defendant's invocation of the Sixth Amendment "misconceive[d]").

APPENDIX A....See Appendix 8

APPENDIX B....See Appendix 9

APPENDIX C

GENERAL COURT-MARTIAL
UNITED STATES COAST GUARD
UNITED STATES
v.
WEBSTER M. SMITH, CADET, U.S. COAST GUARD

FILED UNDER SEAL[*]

MEMORANDUM ORDER AND OPINION

M.R.E. 413 [sic] EVIDENCE
CADET [SR]

The Defense has provided notice that it intends to introduce evidence of specific instances of sexual behavior involving then Cadet, now Ensign [SR]. This alleged sexual behavior is the subject of the secret that Cadet Smith is charged with threatening to expose in Specification I of Additional Charge II. The Government seeks to bar the introduction of such evidence pursuant to M.R.E. 412. At the Article 39(a) session held on 23 May 2006, Ensign [SR] did not testify because she invoked her right under Article 31(b) to consult with an attorney. The accused testified as to the content of his conversations with Cadet [SR] on this subject. The Defense also submitted a written statement dated 15 February 2006 that Cadet [SR] provided to the Coast Guard Investigative Service.

[* Petitioner notes that by order dated October 29, 2009, the court of appeals unsealed this order. Petitioner has nonetheless changed all uses of the accuser's name to her initials.]

FINDINGS OF FACT

248

During the summer training program at the start of their first class year, Cadet Smith and Cadet [SR] were both assigned to patrol boats that moored at Station Little Creek. Both lived in barracks rooms at the Station. In May 2005, Cadet Smith approached Cadet [SR] to inform her that he was hearing rumors from the enlisted personnel assigned to the Station that she had a sexual encounter with an enlisted member assigned to the Station. Cadet [SR] told him that this was true, but that it was not a consensual encounter. Cadet Smith then informed the enlisted personnel who were spreading the rumors that the conduct was not consensual.

On or about 19 October 2005, Cadet Smith again approached Cadet [SR]. He told her that he had remained in contact with some of the enlisted personnel assigned to Station Little Creek and that the rumors surrounding her sexual encounter with the enlisted man had continued. This time she told him that the incident with the enlisted man had been a consensual encounter and that scope of the encounter had been greater than she had previously described.

At the Article 32 hearing, Cadet [SR] merely stated that she had confided a secret to Cadet Smith.

In her 15 February 2006 statement, she merely stated that a situation occurred which led to rumors. On both occasions, she went on to state that on October 19th, she was concerned enough that Cadet Smith would expose this secret that she agreed to pose for a picture with him in which both of them were nude, and later that night allowed him to perform cunnilingus on her then she performed fellatio on him.

CONCLUSIONS OF LAW

1. Generally, evidence that an alleged victim of a sexual offense engaged in other sexual behavior or evidence of the alleged victim's sexual predisposition is not admissible. M.R.E. 412(a). There are three exceptions to this general rule, but only one may be relevant here: evidence of the sexual behavior of the victim is admissible if excluding the evidence would violate the constitutional rights of the accused. M.R.E. 412(b)(1)(C). This exception protects the accused's Sixth Amendment right to confront witnesses and Fifth Amendment right to a fair trial. *United States v. Banker*, 60 M.J. 216, 221 (2004). In other words, the accused has a right to produce relevant evidence that is material and favorable to his defense. *Id.* Evidence is relevant if it tends to make the existence of any fact more or less probable than it would be without the evidence. M.R.E. 401. Assuming these requirements are met, the accused must also demonstrate that the probative value of the evidence outweighs the danger of unfair prejudice. M.R.E. 412(c)(3). In this context, the unfair prejudice is, in part, to the privacy interests of the alleged victim. *Banker*, 60 M.J. at 223. M.R.E. 412 is a legislative recognition of the high value we as a society place on keeping our sexual behavior private.

2. The Defense offered several theories of why this evidence is admissible. First, the Defense wanted to introduce this evidence to impeach the credibility of Ensign [SR] when she testifies. The general rule is that a witness' credibility may be attacked in the form of an opinion or by reputation concerning the witness' character for truthfulness. M.R.E. 608(a). Specific instances of conduct of witness may be admitted, at the discretion of the military judge, if probative of truthfulness.

I decline to exercise that discretion in this case because I believe that, under these circumstances, the probative value of this evidence is substantially outweighed by the danger of unfair prejudice. Then Cadet [SR] was under no duty to be completely forthcoming with Cadet Smith concerning her private life, particularly under these circumstances since her rumored conduct would be in violation of Coast Guard regulations and could subject her to disciplinary action or other adverse consequences. More important, despite any limiting instruction, members might consider this evidence less for its tendency to prove Ensign [SR]'s character for truthfulness than for its tendency to prove that she is a bad person. Finally, conflicting testimony on this point from Ensign [SR] and Cadet Smith could easily sidetrack members from testimony regarding the charged offenses which the member's should be focusing on.

3. The Defense also argued that the members must know the substance of Cadet [SR]'s secret in order for she would feel coerced into taking a nude photograph with Cadet Smith and later engaging in mutual oral sex in order to protect that secret. While the importance of her secret would be relevant in this fashion, I do not think that the members would need to know the specifics. At the Article 39(a) session, the Government offered a generic formulation that would impress upon the members the seriousness of the secret. In essence, the members could be informed that the secret was information that if revealed could have an adverse impact on her Coast Guard career, including possibly disciplinary action under the UCMJ.

4. The final rationale offered by the Defense at the Article 39(a) hearing is the most persuasive. The Defense argued that if the members hear that Cadet [SR] originally told Cadet Smith that a sexual encounter with another man was non-consensual, and then later admitted that it in fact was consensual, then the members could use this testimony to infer that the same thing is happening in this case. In other words, the members could infer that Cadet [SR] has a propensity to bring false accusations against men with whom she has had consensual sexual encounters. I agree that this theory would be a valid reason for admitting this evidence under M.R.E. 412(b)(1)(C), but there are two problems with the Defense proffer. First, the evidence

251

proffered that Cadet [SR] made these statements is not strong since it comes from the accused, who has an obvious bias. Cadet [SR]'s written statement and Article 32 testimony on this point is not clear. She admitted at the Article 32 that she only partially confided in Cadet Smith in May and fully confided in him on October 19th; however, this is far from proof that she initially claimed that the encounter was non-consensual. In fact, it is consistent with the rest of Cadet Smith's Article 39(a) testimony that on October 19th she told him that the /scope of the sexual encounter had been greater than she had previously described. The probative value of this evidence is therefore low.

5. More important, there is no evidence that Cadet [SR] made an official complaint against the unnamed enlisted man. Even if Cadet [SR] told the accused in May that the encounter was not consensual,
the nature of this confidential statement is far different from the nature of her statements to law enforcement personnel that she must have known would result in a public prosecution. Cadet [SR]'s alleged statement to Cadet Smith was apparently intended to keep more people from learning about her sexual encounter with the enlisted man. It was not a false complaint to law enforcement. In contrast, her statements made in this case were to law enforcement personal and would certainly lead to a public prosecution. Consequently, even if Cadet [SR] falsely told the accused *in confidence* that her sexual encounter with the enlisted man was nonconsensual *in an effort to suppress rumors*, this would have little value in proving that her *official* allegations against Cadet Smith *resulting in a public trial* are also false. I am convinced that the minimal probative value of this evidence is outweighed by danger of unfair prejudice to Ensign [SR]'s privacy interests and the potential danger of sidetracking the member's attention to a collateral issue as described in paragraph 2 above.

For the above reasons, the Government's objection that this evidence is inadmissible in accordance with M.R.E. 413 [sic] is SUSTAINED.

EFFECTIVE DATE
This order was effective on 26 May 2006.
Done at Washington, DC,
/s/
Brian Judge
Captain, U.S. Coast Guard
Military Judge

APPENDIX D

IN THE UNITED STATES COAST GUARD
COURT OF CRIMINAL APPEALS
Docket No. 1275
CGCMG 0224
UNITED STATES,
Appellee
v.
WEBSTER M. SMITH, CADET, U.S. COAST GUARD,
Appellant
14 May 2008
APPELLANT'S MOTION FOR RECONSIDERATION EN BANC
FILED 9 MAY 2008

ORDER

Appellant filed a Motion for Reconsideration En
Banc, and for leave to file a brief in support thereof. On consideration of
Appellant's Motion, filed under the Court's Rules of Practice and
Procedure, it is, by the Court, this 14th day of May, 2008, ORDERED:

That Appellant's Motion be, and the same is, hereby denied.

For the Court,
L. I. McClelland
Chief Judge
Copy: Office of Military Justice
Appellate Government Counsel
Appellate Defense Counsel

Appendix 12

Amicus Brief in Support of Supreme Court Appeal from U S Army Defense Appellate Division

No. 10-18

IN THE
SUPREME COURT OF THE UNITED STATES

WEBSTER M. SMITH,

Petitioner,

v.

THE UNITED STATES OF AMERICA,

Respondent,

ON PETITION FOR A WRIT OF CERTIORARI
TO THE UNITED STATES COURT OF
APPEALS FOR THE ARMED FORCES

BRIEF FOR AMICUS CURIAE, UNITED STATES
ARMY DEFENSE APPELLATE DIVISION IN
SUPPORT OF PETITIONER

MARK TELLITOCCI
Colonel, United States Army
Chief, Defense Appellate Division

JESS ROBERTS
Captain, United States Army
Appellate Counsel
Defense Appellate Division

JONATHAN POTTER
Lieutenant Colonel,
United States Army
Senior Appellate
Counsel
Defense Appellate
Division
901 N. Stuart Street
Arlington, VA 22203
(703) 588-6717
jonathan.potter@
conus.army.mil
Counsel of Record

Blank Page

i

QUESTION PRESENTED

When a trial judge's restriction on the cross examination of a prosecution witness is challenged on appeal as a violation of the Confrontation Clause, is the standard of review de novo, as five circuits have held, or abuse of discretion, as six other circuits (and the court of appeals here) have concluded?

TABLE OF CONTENTS

QUESTION PRESENTED..i

TABLE OF AUTHORITIES....................................iii

INTEREST OF AMICUS CURIAE...........................1

INTRODUCTION AND
SUMMARY OF THE ARGUMENT...........................2

REASONS FOR GRANTING
THE PETITION..3

CONCLUSION..8

TABLE OF AUTHORITIES

Cases

Bose Corp. v. Consumers Union of U.S.,
466 U.S. 485 (1984). 7

Constitution, Statutes, and Rules for Courts-Martial

U.S. CONST. amend. VI...2,3

Fed. R. Evid. 412(a) 3

Fed. R. Evid. 412(b)(1)(C)..5

Manual for Courts-Martial,
Mil. R. Evid. 404...6

Manual for Courts-Martial,
Mil. R. Evid. 405...6

Manual for Courts-Martial,
Mil. R. Evid. 412...2,3,5,6,7

Manual for Courts-Martial,
Mil. R. Evid. 412(a) 3,4

Manual for Courts-Martial,
Mil. R. Evid. 412(b)(1)(C) 5

Manual for Courts-Martial,
Mil. R. Evid. 412(c)(1) 4

260

Manual for Courts-Martial,
Mil. R. Evid. 412(c)(2) 4

Manual for Courts-Martial,
Mil. R. Evid. 412(d) 4

Manual for Courts-Martial,
Mil. R. Evid. 413..6

Other Sources

Kerry C. O'Dell,
Criminal Law Chapter: Evidence in Sexual Assault,
7 Geo. J. Gender & L., 819 (2006)..............................3

No. 10-18

WEBSTER M. SMITH,

Petitioner,

v.

THE UNITED STATES OF AMERICA,

Respondent,

ON PETITION FOR A WRIT OF CERTIORARI TO THE UNITED STATES COURT OF APPEALS FOR THE ARMED FORCES

BRIEF FOR AMICUS CURIAE, UNITED STATES ARMY DEFENSE APPELLATE DIVISION IN SUPPORT OF PETITIONER

The United States Army Defense Appellate Division respectfully submits this brief as *amicus curiae* in support of the petitioner.

INTEREST OF AMICUS CURIAE

The United States Army Defense Appellate Division represents individual Soldiers who have been convicted by court-martial and who have been adjudged either a punitive discharge or confinement for one year or more. Defense Appellate Division lawyers, all of whom are Judge Advocates, represent these individuals at the Army Court of Criminal Appeals, the Court of Appeals for the Armed Forces, and the Supreme Court of the United States.[1] The Defense Appellate Division is deeply interested in this case because the relevant standard of review is implicated in virtually every contested sexual assault case litigated by Army appellate lawyers, and is currently at issue in numerous cases before the Army Court of Criminal Appeals and the Court of Appeals for the Armed Forces. The Defense Appellate Division offers the unique perspective of lawyers in the appellate trenches, litigating cases on a daily basis that involve the very issue in this case— the appropriate standard of review for a trial judge's restriction of cross-examination.

INTRODUCTION AND SUMMARY
OF THE ARGUMENT

The petition for certiorari should be granted because the Court of Appeals for the Armed Forces applied an abuse of discretion standard, rather than the correct de novo standard of review. The plain language of Military Rule of Evidence (MRE) 412 indicates that decisions to exclude such evidence have constitutional implications, specifically regarding the Sixth Amendment right to confront

---

[1] No counsel for a party authored this brief in whole or in part, and no person or party, other than *amicus*, its members, or its counsel, made a monetary contribution to the preparation or submission of this brief. Counsel of record for all parties received timely notice of intent to file and have consented to the filing of this brief.

witnesses, thus making a de novo standard of review appropriate.

The Army Defense Appellate Division agrees with the petitioner's argument that evidentiary questions that implicate Sixth Amendment and other constitutional claims should be reviewed de novo. The Defense Appellate Division's experience has generally been with the specific rule of evidence at issue in petitioner's case—MRE 412. Thus, the Defense Appellate Division's brief will explain that rule's implementation in courts-martial and demonstrate that MRE 412 and similar statutes in the civilian realm are a different sort of animal from other evidentiary rules, presenting a need for the extra protection afforded by de novo review.

REASONS FOR GRANTING THE PETITION

Military of Rule of Evidence 412 mirrors Federal Rule of Evidence (FRE) 412, which is also followed by ten states. Kerry C. O'Dell, *Criminal Law Chapter: Evidence in Sexual Assault*, 7 Geo. J. Gender & L., 819, 831 (2006). All fifty states and the District of Columbia have statutes that exclude the purported victim's consensual sexual activity with third parties. *Id.* at 820. Military Rule of Evidence 412 and similar statutes are exclusionary rules; so-called "rape shield" laws that place the sexual behaviors of an alleged victim of a sexual offense beyond the limits of relevancy. *See* Mil. R. Evid. 412(a); Fed. R. Evid. 412(a).

According to the language of MRE 412, any evidence of the "sexual behavior" or "sexual predispositions" of an alleged victim are forbidden from being entered into evidence. Mil. R. Evid. 412(a). Military Rule of Evidence 412(d) defines "sexual behavior" as any behavior that is sexual in nature outside of the charged offense. Mil. R. Evid. 412(d). This same section defines "sexual predisposition" as the alleged victim's "mode of dress, speech, or lifestyle that does not directly refer to sexual activities but that may have a sexual connotation." *Id.* The classic example is that MRE 412 would prevent the admission of evidence that an alleged victim habitually dressed provocatively, as though to say he or she invited the assault.

The rule prescribes strict procedures when contemplating admitting such evidence; not to protect the accused, but to protect the purported victim from potentially humiliating evidentiary arguments in open court. *See* Mil. R. Evid. 412(c)(1). The rule requires notice of the evidence to be offered be given to parties and the court at least five days before pleas are entered. *Id.* This notice must state both the nature of the evidence and the precise purpose for which it is being offered. *Id.* A closed hearing is then conducted outside the view of both the fact-finding panel and the public during which the parties may call witnesses and be heard regarding the admission of the evidence. Mil. R. Evid. 412(c)(2). Thus, the rule prescribes a mini-trial solely for the purpose of determining the evidence's admissibility.

Military Rule of Evidence 412 contemplates that evidence of "sexual behaviors" or "predispositions" might survive this closed hearing process and be deemed admissible under three exceptions. It is the third, MRE 412(b)(1)(C), that is by far the most litigated in military trials and appeals. This exception applies for "evidence the exclusion of which would violate the constitutional rights of the accused." Mil. R. Evid. 412(b)(1)(C). It is identical in form and function to FRE 412 and the prevailing rules in a number of other jurisdictions. *See, e.g.,* Fed. R. Evid. 412(b)(1)(C). In the Defense Appellate Division's experience, every case implicating MRE 412 since 2006 has revolved upon this "constitutional rights" exception.

The "constitutional rights" exception to MRE 412 clearly brings the question of an accused's constitutional entitlements to the forefront of any ruling in which MRE 412 is used to exclude evidence. The exception is an acknowledgement of the fact that a rule which limits an accused's ability to confront witnesses, present a defense, and have his or her matter heard in a public trial must be wielded with extreme caution. Special attention must be paid to the tension between the legitimate protection of victims and the potential for a broad manner of application that destroys the constitutional protections of an accused. A judicial authority, by negative implication of MRE 412(b)(1)(C), must weigh an accused's constitutional rights in every case in which evidence regarding such an alleged victim is sought.

"Rape shield" rules are exceptions to the general
precepts of relevant evidence and so warrant the
heightened protections offered by de novo review. *Cf.*
Mil. R. Evid. 405 (codifying the typical approach to
relevant character evidence). One of the side-effects
of MRE 412 is to prevent otherwise relevant and
admissible evidence that may be critical to the
defense from being presented to the fact-finder.
When combined with MRE 413, which allows
comparable evidence about the accused to be
presented to the fact-finder, MRE 412 creates the
anomalous result whereby the government is
statutorily permitted to present a much broader
range of evidence than the defense in sexual assault
trials. *See* Mil. R. Evid. 413. Military Rule of
Evidence 413 allows the admission of "evidence of
the accused's commission of one or more offenses of
sexual assault," with very few subject matter or
temporal limitations, effectively making any prior
sexual offense charge relevant, admissible evidence.
The effect of this rule is an exception to the MRE 404
ban on character evidence being used to prove
propensity, found in both the Military and Federal
Rules of Evidence. *See* Mil. R. Evid. 413, 404.

Under MRE 412 and 413, for example, the
government can present evidence of any sexual
assault charge from the accused's past as evidence on
the merits, but the defense is not allowed to present
evidence that the alleged victim frequently fabricates
sexual assault accusations. *See generally* Mil. R.
Evid. 412, 413. The constitutional implications of
such a scenario are clear and warrant close judicial
scrutiny to ensure that justice is served. Thus, a de
novo standard of review ensures that the rights of an

accused are balanced with the rights of the purported victim.

The adoption of de novo review would not require an appellate judge to re-try every evidentiary ruling made by the trial court. *See Bose Corp. v. Consumers Union of U.S.*, 466 U.S. 485 (1984). It would simply grant the appellate courts the power and ability to come to a different conclusion regarding an evidentiary ruling than the trial court below without having to extend deference to the trial court. *Id.* To authorize the de novo standard for cases such as this would merely allow an independent inquiry into whether a trial judge's ruling was sufficient to protect an accused's constitutional interests in an area of the law where they are particularly threatened.

A de novo standard is the appropriate standard of review in cases such as this. After all, MRE 412 and other "rape shield" statutes implicate constitutional issues, but they do so in a closed hearing that is essentially a mini-trial. Considering the complexity of such proceedings and the grave nature of the issues at stake, de novo review is appropriate. Indeed, logic demands that de novo review is necessary.

CONCLUSION

The Petition for Certiorari should be granted.

Respectfully submitted,

MARK TELLITOCCI
Colonel, United States Army
Chief, Defense Appellate
   Division

JESS B. ROBERTS
Captain, United States Army
Appellate Counsel
Defense Appellate Division

JONATHAN POTTER
Lieutenant Colonel,
United States Army
Senior Appellate
   Counsel
Defense Appellate
   Division
901 N. Stuart Street
Arlington, VA 22203
(703) 588-6717
jonathan.potter@
   conus.army.mil
Counsel of Record

269

Appendix 13

Decision of Supreme Court Without Comment Denying Certiorari

IN THE SUPREME COURT OF THE UNITED STATES OF AMERICA

No. 10-18

Title:Webster M. Smith, Petitioner

v.

United States

Docketed:June 30, 2010

Lower Ct:United States Court of Appeals for the Armed Forces

Case Nos.:(08-0719)

Decision Date:March 29, 2010

Date ~~~ Proceedings and Orders

- Jun 28 2010 Petition for a writ of certiorari filed. (Response due July 30, 2010)

- Jul 21 2010 Order extending time to file response to petition to and including August 30, 2010.

- Jul 30 2010 Brief amicus curiae of National Association of Criminal Defense Lawyers filed.

- Jul 30 2010 Brief amicus curiae of United States Army Defense Appellate Division filed.

- Aug 23 2010 Order further extending time to file response to petition to and including September 29, 2010.

- Sep 22 2010 Order further extending time to file response to petition to and including October 28, 2010.

- Oct 28 2010 Brief of respondent United States in opposition filed.

- Nov 5 2010 Reply of petitioner Webster M. Smith filed. TBP

- Nov 8 2010 DISTRIBUTED for Conference of November 23, 2010.

- Nov 29 2010 Petition DENIED.

Name~~~~~~~~~~~~~~   Address~~~~~~~~~~~~~~~Phone~~~
Attorneys for Petitioner:

Daniel S. Volchok, Wilmer Cutler Hale and Dorr LLP(202) 663-6000
1875 Pennsylvania Avenue, NW
Washington, DC 20006
Party name: Webster M. Smith
Attorneys for Respondent:
Neal Kumar Katyal, Acting Solicitor General(202) 514-2217
United States Department of Justice
950 Pennsylvania Avenue, N.W.
Washington, DC 20530-0001
SupremeCtBriefs@USDOJ

Party name: United States

Other:
Jonathan L. Marcus, Covington & Burling, LLP(202) 662-6000
1201 Pennsylvania Avenue, NW
Washington, DC 20004
jmarcus@cov.com
Party name: National Association of Criminal Defense Lawyers

Jonathan F. Potter, Senior Appellate Counsel United States Army(703) 588-6717
Defense Appellate Division
901 N. Stuart Street
Arlington, VA 22203
jonathan.potter@conus.army.mil
Party name: United States Army Defense Appellate Division

Made in the USA
Charleston, SC
27 April 2011